CHILTERN VILLAGES

HISTORY, PEOPLE AND PLACES
in the
CHILTERN HILLS

CHILTERN VILLAGES

History, People and Places
in the
Chiltern Hills

VERA BURDEN

SPURBOOKS LIMITED

Published by

SPURBOOKS LTD.

1 Station Road,
Bourne End,
Buckinghamshire

Printed in Great Britain by
Redwood Press Limited
Trowbridge, Wiltshire

SBN 0 902875 21 3

Contents

Illustrations

The photographs on pages 41, 69, 70, 75, 85, 108, are reproduced with the kind permission of The National Portrait Gallery. All other photographs are by Eric Burden.

Apart from those listed above, the photographs are the copyright of the author.

Cover picture by Raymond Lea.

ACKNOWLEDGMENTS

Acknowledgment is made to the *Bucks Examiner* for their courtesy in allowing me to draw upon articles of mine printed from 1970–72.

I am most grateful to those many people who answered my questions and helped me with their local knowledge. In every village I found friendly help, and time willingly given. Thanks are due to the Rector of Princes Risborough and the Rector of Aston Rowant for permission to use extracts from their churchwardens' accounts. Especially I wish to express my gratitude to the staff of the Barham Park Library, Brent, for their patience and ready assistance, to Paddy Burley for reading the manuscript and checking historical facts, to Rose Rogers for her admirable work on the typescript, and my sons, Peter and Nicholas, for assistance with items of natural history. Finally, without the encouragement and unfailing support of Eric, who held the camera, the book would never have been written.

INTRODUCTION

Opinions vary as to the precise limits of the Chilterns, but for the purpose of this book I have taken them as ranging roughly from Goring and Ewelme in the west to Chenies and the Gaddesdens in the east. The steep escarpment of the higher hills to the west forms a fairly recognisable boundary, whereas to the east, where the lower slopes dwindle towards Middlesex and the Colne Valley, it is much more difficult to say where the Chilterns cease. The area I have covered is, with the exception of Goring in Oxfordshire and Waterend in Hertfordshire, contained within the Ordnance Survey Map, The Chilterns, Sheet 159. I have tried to cover the selected area comprehensively, but being more concerned with the hills than the river, have only touched briefly on the riverside towns.

Local legends and personalities are part of the essence of every village. I have had no hesitation in indulging in tales which have been passed down from one generation to another, or in relating traditional customs and beliefs. These, like local names and the evocative details of parish records, lend colour to the story of each and every village.

Fast travel has enabled people to work in the city and live in the contrasting peace of the countryside. Contemporary country-dwellers are not all country people. While there is no denying the major roads and motorways under construction, and in prospect, the realisation is at last dawning that development and roads should be moulded into the landscape and not slapped across it. The people of the Chilterns are fighting hard to stem the tide of spoilation of the natural features.

In describing the villages I have concentrated on their visual charm and their historical associations. This is a personal view of the Chilterns, and if my own enthusiasms and preferences do not always coincide with yours I must ask to be forgiven. I have visited all the places of which I have written and, whilst only too well aware of the rapidity with which the scene changes, I can only say that the information given is correct, as far as I know, at the time of going to press.

BUCKINGHAMSHIRE

CHAPTER I

Turville to Fawley

The unpretentious hills of the Chilterns are within an hour's journey of London. They shelter villages and hamlets which, still holding their own against the invasive tide of development, have an air of reassuring tranquillity. Such villages are to be found throughout the entire length and breadth of the Chilterns. They have no set pattern. Checkendon and Great Hampden repose in secluded woodland; Aldbury, on the north-eastern boundary, and Stonor to the west, shelter below a protective ridge; others like Penn perch on a high spur. A few, which once answered to the name village, have grown beyond recognition to acquire a new face, as Beaconsfield and Amersham have done.

Each has its own individual appeal; and Turville, deeply hidden in the long Hambleden Valley, has the timeless air which is typical of the more remote of these Chiltern villages. It is as if they have gone into retirement after the more strenuous days of a bygone age. Occasionally it is possible to arrive in Turville and find no one of its small population in sight, though the impression that everyone is asleep or has made an exodus to the nearest town rarely lasts more than a minute or two. A tractor will appear trundling its way along the narrow road, a dog runs to and fro, uncertain whether he should be before or behind, a girl sets off to cycle to the nearest shop at Skirmett and the whole village is astir.

Turville's brick and timbered cottages, its picturesque Bull and Butcher Inn, and its compact little Norman Church are gathered about the green. A green only just large enough for the High Wycombe bus to manoeuvre its way round for its return journey. Rising to the north of this closely collected group is the steep slope of Turville Hill.

On its crest stands a twelve-sided windmill of the type known as a smock-mill, because its weatherboarding was worn like a woman's smock or shift. Sail-less, known as Cobstone Mill and now occupied as a private house, it is a distinctive landmark 500 feet above sea level. Indeed so totally withdrawn into its Chiltern "bottom" is the rest of the village that

1. *Turville Smock Mill*

from the hills to the south-west the mill is the only visible sign of its existence.

It gazes down upon the lazy smoke weaving up above the lichened roofs. Beyond, a long white chalk track charges up to meet the beechwoods. In the middle ages and earlier these woods, and those of the whole Chiltern area, gave refuge to outlaws and men seeking escape from justice and persecution. Following William the Conqueror's major victory at Hastings parties of fleeing Saxons, by no means entirely subdued, found cover in the wild and mostly uninhabited forests.

On the tracks travelling along the valley to Watlington and Oxford small Norman garrisons were established. Turville may well mark the site of one such encampment and it is believed that the ditch around the vicarage garden indicates where a fort was set up. Long after the Normans and Saxons had settled down to live at peace together the Chiltern forests continued to be the territory of refugees and men who lived at variance with the law. There was no peace here then; it was an area of trouble consistent and extensive enough to necessitate the appointment of a Steward of the Chiltern Hundreds. His unenviable job was to ride over

2. *Armorial Window, Turville*

the tracks, searching for the outlaws, catching and hanging them for their misdeeds. By the 18th century the Steward's duties had long since become outdated and it was in 1750 that the office of the Chiltern Hundreds was first granted to members of Parliament as grounds for resignation.

It was as an exile that the French General, Charles Dumouriez, came to live at Turville Park, the large rambling house on Turville Heath; he had fled from France shortly after the execution of Louis XVI in 1792, and was to spend the rest of his life until his death in 1823 in Turville. Dumouriez was not the only refugee from the French Revolution to receive shelter in the Chilterns, for in Penn a school was established by Edmund Burke for fatherless French children. The school is no longer there, but for many years afterwards the field in which it stood was known as French School Meadow.

Turville's little church of St. Mary holds many reminders of people who have lived and worshipped here. Monuments commemorate the lords of the manor and their families in accordance with past custom. More exceptionally there is a great window composed of armorial glass of the 16th and 17th centuries showing the arms of the Dudley, Sidney and Perry families. In the reign of Elizabeth I Philip Sidney, knight and man of letters, and his uncle Robert Dudley, Earl of Leicester and a favourite of the Queen, gave their names a permanent place in English history. Elizabeth Sidney, a descendant of Sir Philip, married William Perry, a Sheriff of Buckinghamshire and the builder of Turville Park.

When the Rev. John Charlesworth came to the parish in 1947 he discovered some further fragments of similar glass adorning the front door of the vicarage. He had them removed from what he thought to be a somewhat dangerous position to the safety of the church. They are now set into the south windows, and one of them poses a small mystery. It commemorates the marriage of Humphrey Clarke and Mary Marcham, but is unique for her surname has been partially scratched out and reads, "Mary Ma—". Guessing why, or by whom, her name was erased is one of the two unsolved mysteries of Turville. During restoration work in 1900 a huge stone coffin was dug up beneath the church floor. On being opened it was seen to contain two burials, one of whom was a female with a small hole in her skull. Sensational newsmen were quick to exploit the possibilities of an undetected crime. Anyone was free to offer an explanation, but against the melodramatic suggestions of foul play is the more rational thought that in mediaeval days it was not unusual for old graves to be re-opened for the interment of the newly deceased. Despite an exhaustive search through village records no mention was found of any

3. *Mary Marcham Window*

unexplained disappearance of a woman of that time. Who she was, and the cause of the hole in her skull remains unknown.

On the doorway I noticed the two inch long Pilgrims' Crosses cut into the stonework. These began in the 14th century and each one recorded the saying of a Requiem Mass for a parishioner who had died away from home, probably in battle.

A cottage has ventured into the churchyard, and The Old Vicarage, no longer serving its intended purpose, has an attractive Gothic affinity with the buildings of coloured bricks made by children in the pre-plastic age. There are still a handful of pensioners living hereabouts who can recall a stream which once ran beside it, but of which there is now no trace. Many a village has, as Turville does, both an old and a new vicarage. The church gains from the sale of a house designed to accommodate not only the vicar and his wife and family, but also the staff needed to run it; whilst the present day clergy gain a home more fitting to contemporary circumstances.

The Hambleden Valley and the western edge of the Chilterns are some of its most secluded areas, and Turville's continuing remoteness is partially due to the surrounding beechwoods. Their leaf-strewn paths are still a place of refuge for anyone who wishes to escape from the mechanised clamour of the metropolis.

Walk up through the Dolesden Valley to Southend and before you go on to Stonor Park you will see a collection of ornamental wildfowl wandering in comparative freedom in the gardens of The Drover. A path on this route bears a courteous request that not only dogs, but all pets should be kept on a lead. Climb the turfed slopes, where the whitebeam grows, to pass Cobstone Mill, drop swiftly down through Mill Hanging Wood and a bridleway will take you to Cadmore End.

The Chilterns abound in "Ends". In Cadmore End the village store has been unable to resist calling itself "The Absolute End". The village was once a part of Fingest, but became a separate parish in 1866. The Old Ship Inn, the Old Post Office and the school occupy the north side of the road, and on the south the rest of the village straggles about a haphazard series of little commons. A wooden seat circles an old oak like a frill; a group of lanky Scots firs adjoin the church and a cottage where once girls were taught to make lace has a well in its front garden and a donkey in the back.

In the time of Queen Anne about a quarter of Buckinghamshire's total population was employed in the making of lace. Village children from the age of six or seven would receive instruction from their mothers. In the daytime and when it was warm enough the lace-makers would sit at their doorways or even outside. Light was essential to their intricate craft, and an ingenious method was devised to give maximum light to a maximum number of workers. A candle was placed in the centre of a tall three-legged stool. Around it were four glass flasks with spherical tops, and these when filled with snow water acted as lens or condensers, throwing a direct beam of light on to their work. This enabled four women to work by the light of a single candle. With the introduction of machine-made goods following the industrial revolution the demand for hand-made lace dwindled rapidly.

A wider area of common land, and a favourite spot for picnickers, is Turville Heath reached by either road or footpath going directly west from Turville. Bordered by a decorative array of cottages, it is overlooked by Turville Grange. This gracious reminder of more spacious Georgian days was the home of the third Viscount Esher, who amongst his numerous cultural activities was a life president of the Society for the Protection of Ancient Buildings.

Ibstone, too, stretches itself along the edge of heathland studded with golden gorse and bracken. Lying north of the windmill (which is sometimes referred to as Ibstone Mill) and on that same spine of the hills, it boasts a superb view over the Hambleden Valley. And on all the highways and by-ways linking up these villages there is a constant vista of pastoral scenery; open meadows where, in this area of the Chilterns, sheep still graze; more ordered fields under cultivation and the ever-beautiful beech clothing the hills. Willowherb, that fast invader of waste ground, fills the clearings with colour, and the beauty of the bright, golden ragwort belies its name.

A writer, and admirer of the Chilterns, once stated that he would calmly sacrifice Fingest if by doing so Turville remained inviolate. All who know and appreciate Fingest would hasten to its defence in no uncertain terms. Sir William Connor, who both lived in and loved the village, paid countless tributes to its individuality. It was he who, under the name Cassandra, contributed a popular column to a daily newspaper for many years.

Only a mile of winding lane divides Fingest from Turville; both have roots going far back into history, yet each has retained its own separate appeal. Records of Fingest date from Saxon times and its name has had innumerable variations. The Subsidy Roll for 1524 names it as Thynkhurst, and at other times it was Thengest, Vengest and Thinghurst, all of which stemmed from "pinghyrst", meaning "the wooded hill where the assembly met". The manor was part of the demesne of Edward the Confessor and between 1163 and 1547 was held by the Bishops of Lincoln

4. *Fingest Valley*

who are believed to have actually resided in the village. Argument over common land is part of history and was a major problem in the 18th century, but a dispute between villagers and the Bishop occurred in Fingest as early as 1330.

It had interesting consequences being the basis of a ghost story which could have been a cunning method of ensuring that an area of common was restored to the village people. Henry de Burghers, Bishop of Lincoln in 1330, had a licence to impark three hundred acres of land adjoining his own property. Inevitably this encroachment was deeply resented by the village and complaints were rife. After the Bishop's death in 1343 it was said that his ghost appeared, distraught and in the dress of a forester. As punishment for the hardship he had caused he was doomed to act as a keeper of the park until restitution had been made. The Canons of Lincoln were so affected by his plea that they had dividing hedges uprooted and ditches filled in. I assume the Bishop was then allowed to rest in peace.

The small collection of houses and cottages now composing this very small village is dominated by the great 60 foot tower of the Norman church. Of formidable strength it looks ready to withstand all eventuali-

5. *Fingest Church*

ties. The twin gables at the top, forming its striking and renowned saddle-back roof, were added about 400 years after the Normans built the 4 foot thick walls on which it rests.

About 100 yards along Chequers Lane, and past Church Cottage with its curiously tall chimney, are the well preserved railings of Fingest Parish Pound within which stray animals used to be confined.

A favourite view of the village is from the entrance to Fingest and Mousell's Wood on the hills to the south-east towards Frieth. The climb is short, though steep, and the way is frequently muddy, but with a few careful steps the mud can be by-passed and it takes no more than fifteen minutes to reach the top. There is the village deep in its hollow calm and unperturbed, the unique tower still in full view. Cattle graze peace-fully in the fields and on the opposite hillside, below Hanger Wood, sheep string out over the grass, their repetitive cries lessening as they return to their cropping of the turf.

Wandering on from this viewpoint the woodland path leads to the hamlet of Frieth. A village which climbs a hill and where everything, except for the massive topiaried yew of the inn, seems to be on a small scale. School, cottages, village hall—all are small. Even the Victorian church has neither tower nor steeple, not even a bell-turret.

Between Fingest and Hambleden are three miles of valley bordered by beechwoods, and as it meets the Thames there is the white-timbered Hambleden Mill, one of the 5,624 watermills recorded in Domesday, when it was worth an annual rent of £1. Entrance to the waterside is on foot only, and a car park is provided along the Hambleden Road. As you cross the narrow footway there is the dramatic contrast of gushing water and the clear reflections in the still river beyond. The last time I was there green umbrellas sheltering silent anglers dotted the banks where the willows hang over the water and expert canoeists were performing exercises about the weir.

One of the comparatively few places to so far provide proof of Roman settlement in the Chilterns is here at Mill End. In 1911 the site of a Roman villa was excavated near Yewden Manor. A mosaic floor and a great storage jar for grain featured amongst the finds. The large number of small, everyday objects also discovered seem to me even more fascinat-ing. There were pins used for fastening clothes, hairpins and needles, simple brooches, tools, spoons and a tiny open-ended bracelet a child could have worn. Until recently there was a small museum in Hambleden which housed many of these relics. Regrettably it is now closed and the contents, on loan from Viscount Hambleden, have been transferred to the County Museum at Aylesbury.

Away to the west, also by the river, is Greenlands, a Victorian mansion built in 1853. It was the home of W. H. Smith who became a household name through his newsagency business. This remarkable man, born in 1825, the son of strict Methodists, wanted to become a priest but went into the family business in deference to his father's wishes. He expanded the business with enormous success and by 1862 had secured the exclusive right to erect bookstalls on all the important railway stations in England. He insisted that pernicious literature, for which these bookstalls had been notorious, was to be excluded. Reaching high office in the Government he was universally respected for his integrity and thorough kindness of heart. It was in recognition of his service that a peerage, with the title Viscountess Hambleden, was conferred on his widow after his death in 1891.

Businessmen now confer in his old home, and the large area of 4,500 acres known as the Greenlands estate is protected by the National Trust. It includes the village which, situated one mile north of the mill, is watered by the River Hamble, one of the five small rivers of the southern half of Buckinghamshire.

Hambleden has associations with many famous men. In the 13th century the manor belonged to the Count of Evreux, and after his death

6. Hambleden Village Store

passed to his widow, Millicent. Her second marriage was to William de Canteloupe, and one of their sons, Thomas, born in 1218, was to become Hambleden's most eminent son. As Bishop of Hereford he fought corruption and helped the poor, and was for a while advisor to Edward I. An ecclesiastical disagreement with his Archbishop led to him being excommunicated, and before his case could be heard by the Pope, he died. It was not long before the news circulated that miracles had occurred at his tomb in Hereford Cathedral. Even for those credulous days the number of such miracles was deemed to be remarkable, and resulted, not surprisingly, in his canonisation in 1320.

His likeness may be seen in a window of the Lady Chapel in Hambleden's church. This chapel, now refitted through the generosity of the Hambleden family, was once known as The Sheepfold; a homely name which arose because here sat the farm hands who came to services in their working dress, and the floor beneath their feet was strewn with straw. That this was, and still is, a farming community is reflected in some of the old local names such as Rakestrawe and Shipwash (or Sheepwash).

The church contains a rich store of varied treasures. There is an oak muniment chest once the property of Lord Cardigan who commanded the heroic Charge of the Light Brigade at Balaclava; a modern crucifix designed by Anthony Foster, a local artist from Frieth and a pupil of Eric Gill, and a nave altar famed for being constructed from a 15th century bedhead used by Cardinal Wolsey. Two of Hambleden's bells are said to have been cast from two won by a former rector from his Fingest colleague at cards.

Parish records are both a reliable and an intriguing source of local information. The Churchwardens' accounts frequently included payment for the destruction of creatures regarded as pests. Hambleden's accounts mention polecats and hedgehogs. Polecats, now confined to the isolated regions of Wales, would have caused havoc in a poultry yard, but what harm the hedgehog did I fail to understand. His diet of beetles, worms and slugs seems wholly innocuous. Round about 200 years ago many villages had Sparrow Clubs. Money was paid out for dead birds, about 2d. or 3d. a dozen being the usual sum. In 1830 Weston Turville, a mile or so north of Wendover, was paying out as much as $\frac{1}{2}$d. each, but by 1870 the practice had more or less ceased throughout the country.

From the square, jackdaws can be heard chattering about the turreted church tower where, not one, but four weathervanes move in the wind. In the surrounding farmland the crops ripen and are harvested, and each year great sheaves of oats, barley and wheat, saved from mechanical harvesting to be cut especially by hand, are carried by the people in procession through the lych-gate and into the Harvest Festival. The custom has been observed every September for at least 600 years and it remains a fitting gesture of gratitude for a successful harvest.

All over Hambleden there is the pleasing traditional partnership of brick and flint, and it is even repeated in the miniature bridge crossing the Hamble as it flows on through the meadows. Two stores, a butcher, and the comfortable Stag and Huntsman, serve the small population, many of whom are employed on the Hambleden estate. Having escaped the current tendency towards sophistication, it is unquestionably one of the most attractive of all Chiltern villages.

To the east of the square, at the foot of Pheasant's Hill, is the many-gabled manor house, graced by one of the most glorious copper beech I have ever seen. From the top of the hill, before the road bends round to Rockwell End, there is a fine view. In winter chalk streaks the furrowed fields, but even at that time of the year when the trees have lost their screening foliage, there is still no man-made addition to the landscape in sight.

Back in the village the clear little river speeds past the shop, the old pump in the square is shaded by a chestnut tree, and the road by-passes it all and shoots away to join the Henley road leaving Hambleden in peaceful seclusion below the beechwoods.

So renowned are its beechwoods that Buckinghamshire and beech are almost synonymous. Yet it is only in comparatively modern times that the beech has been accepted as native to this country. Authentic proof in the form of beech-charcoal identified as coming from pre-Roman England has at last put paid to the belief that it was a species introduced by Caesar's troops. Less folklore is attached to the beech than to most other British trees. Power against evil has always been attributed to the yew. That the oak is an emblem of fortitude is common knowledge. A sprig of holly may protect your house against lightning, but to bring elder indoors is to invite the Devil to live with you! Nevertheless, Miller in his gardener's dictionary of 1741 remarked that the shade of the beech "is thought to be very salubrious to human bodies". Whatever his reasons for this theory, history has shown that the Chiltern beechwoods have been places of inspiration for poets like Waller and Shelley, of relaxation for statesmen like Burke and Disraeli, and have sheltered individualists like Hampden, Penn and Ellwood. In more recent times, after the end of World War One, when Lord Lee of Fareham gave Chequers to the nation as a country retreat for its prime ministers, he expressed the hope that two days a week in the pure air of the Chiltern hills would benefit both the minister and the country!

The A 4155 sweeping around to Henley passes Fawley Court on its way. The imposing red brick mansion, seen clearly from the road, has an assembly of outbuildings which are not beautiful, but the house itself, despite some indications of faded glory, is of interest.

On this very site stood the home of Sir Bulstrode Whitelocke who served under Cromwell. He was a true man of the Chilterns, his father, Sir James Whitelocke, was "a stout and learned judge" and his mother, Elizabeth, was one of the Bulstrodes of Hedgerley, near Gerrard's Cross. In 1971, a portrait of Sir Bulstrode was rediscovered in a convent in Ireland by Ruth Spalding when researching for a radio programme. It has now been acquired by the National Portrait Gallery.

His house was ransacked by Royalist troops during the Civil War and the present house, since 1952 occupied by the Order of Marian Fathers, was built for William Freeman. Above the main door is an inscription "Wren fecit 1684". According to Pevsner, Wren may well have had a hand in designing it but much of the detail is the work of others.

Fawley is a scattered district of sudden dips, steep climbs, and single track roads—and some that are not so marked but could be. They twist through unspoiled woodland, its floor russet brown with beech leaves. There are farms and cows, and as you round a corner, unexpected fields behind good thick hedgerows. The inn, The Walnut Tree, with its very large garden, is unexpectedly spacious for so small a village. And in the church is a pink and grey marble font and a handsome pulpit carved with cherub's heads. Their presence at Fawley is due to John Freeman, who rebuilt the church in 1748 and brought these fittings from the Duke of Chandos' Palace at Canons, in Middlesex.

As the A 4155 moves on to Henley and Oxfordshire it arrives at the junction of three counties, for the Island Temple below Fawley Court and the starting point of the Henley Regatta is claimed by Berkshire, whilst Fawley remains on the Buckinghamshire side of the county boundary.

CHAPTER II
Wycombe to Hughenden

Wood turning was one of the earliest of Chiltern crafts. Men worked away in the beechwoods on primitive pole-lathes to produce the thin legs and sticks for the chairs for which the area, and High Wycombe in particular, became renowned. Locally they were known as bodgers, men who began a job which other craftsmen finished.

The story of Wycombe is of great antiquarian and historical interest for it was ideally suited to early settlers. Even to-day the site of a hill-top camp, sprouting beech and rising to about 30 ft., is clearly seen in the grounds of Castle Hill House, now housing the Town Museum.

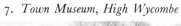

7. Town Museum, High Wycombe

Wycombe's advantageous position in a wide valley between the well-wooded hills and with its own river, the Wye, ensured that by the time the Normans came it was already a sizeable community with 6 mills, 30 ploughs, and 500 pigs which wandered freely in the hillside woods feeding on the beech-mast. Great use has been made of the Wye as it journeys from the Wycombes to Loudwater and on to join the Thames. Watermills have given way to paper mills and factories, but this minor stream has been essential to all of them. The historian Lipscomb suggests that "the noise incessantly made by the rapidity of the stream which rushes with great impetuosity towards Wooburn" was the origin of the name Loudwater.

Neighbouring villages were dependent on Wycombe, not only for employment in the chair-making industry, but also as a market town and as a place to which men came to be hired. A scale of charges for the rent of the market stalls in the year 1874 may still be seen in the Market Hall which Robert Adam built opposite Keene's Guildhall. On payment of £3 a year a man might display his wares on a stall in the covered market, or in the open market for only £2. Farmers and labourers would ride or walk in to the hiring fair from outlying districts. Shepherds would wear a scrap of sheep's wool in their hats, carters and ploughmen a piece

8. Guildhall, High Wycombe

25

9. Church Loft, West Wycombe

of whipcord and the cowmen a cow's hair. Showing these emblems of their trade the farm-hands had to stand about waiting to be hired. Once a bargain had been sealed by payment of one shilling, the hired-hand would place a piece of ribbon in his hat.

When Queen Victoria came through Wycombe in 1877 on her way to visit her Prime Minister and friend, Disraeli, part of the town's welcoming decorations included a great archway of chairs on which was written "God bless the Queen". So impressive was this elaborate structure that the Queen stopped her carriage to look at it more closely. But Wycombe, now the largest town in the Buckinghamshire Chilterns, with its multi-storey car park and shops and offices blotting the sky-line, is no longer a place to dally in and we will leave it by the A 40 to reach the village which shares its name, its river, but not its industrial development.

West Wycombe is a unique place. In 1929 the Royal Society of Arts, whose immediate concern at that time was the preservation of ancient cottages as an integral part of the English countryside, bought up the greater part of the village. Cottages lining the village street, where Tudor, Queen Anne and Georgian architecture seem moulded into one coherent whole, were restored under the supervision of William Weir and in 1934 West Wycombe was presented to the National Trust as an un-spoilt English village.

Yet, the village as an entity is overshadowed by the spectacular church and mausoleum, and the famous, and some would say infamous, caves. All of which came into being through the extravagant and highly imaginative mind of the 18th century knight, Sir Francis Dashwood.

10. *The Mausoleum, West Wycombe*

27

His church on the hill dominates the scene. It has a fine position by any standards for the hill overlooks the meeting point of three long valleys. Cars weave their way up the steep approach where horses once brought their owners to attend morning service whilst they were rested in the adjoining stables. To complement the richly ornate church Dashwood built, to the east of it, the strangest sight of all, the Mausoleum. Built of flint, in 1763, the year in which Dashwood became Lord le Despencer, the hexagonal structure is open to the sky. Urns and monuments are set into the niches and shelves and it resembles a huge, fantastic folly. On payment of a small fee you can, should you wish, wander around inside. It faces Wycombe Park, but the yellow-stuccoed house is now almost entirely obscured by trees.

Half-way down the hill are The Caves, a dramatic excavation going a quarter of a mile into the chalk. A decorative flint entrance, like a sham ruin, underlines the sense of showmanship so characteristic of all Dashwood's architectural undertakings. The caves consist of winding passages and side-chambers, but because of suggestions that they were the scene of the dubious orgies of the 18th century libertines who comprised the Medmenham Hell-Fire Club, their original purpose is frequently overlooked. Dashwood instigated the project to give work to the unemployed of the village, and to procure chalk for the construction of a new road—that straightest of straight roads connecting the village with High Wycombe.

To mark the road's completion a stone pillar was set up at the eastern end of the village. Known locally as "The Pedestal" it bears the date 1752 and in comparison with the modern signpost alongside is parochial in its information, giving the distance from "The Capital", "The University" and "The County Town".

Finally we come to Wycombe Park, the most inspired of Sir Francis' creations, and still the home of the Dashwood family. Their association with West Wycombe began in 1698 when two brothers, Francis and Samuel Dashwood, sons of a Turkey merchant and both aldermen of London, purchased the manor and rectory. Seven years later Francis, on being made a baronet, bought up his brother's half-share. He was the founder of the West Wycombe family and it was his son, born in 1705 and also named Francis, who is remembered for his independent actions, and as a founder member of the Dilettanti Society. He was a wealthy man, travelled widely, was an active member of Parliament for twenty-two years and an outstanding benefactor to the people of West Wycombe.

Over a period of time he transformed his father's plain house, adding a magnificent colonnade to the south front and classical porticos to the

11. *The Pedestal, West Wycombe*

east and west sides. A three day fête was held in the grounds of Wycombe Park in 1771 to celebrate the completion of the west portico, and there was a procession ending by the lake from which a frigate fired salutes. Dashwood's friend, Revett, had modelled the portico on the Temple of Bacchus at Teos, near Smyrna. In the same year that Revett was beautifying Dashwood's home, James Wyatt was building the Island Temple at Fawley Court for Sambroke Freeman, also a member of the Dilettanti Society.

Humphry Repton, the country squire who, because of financial difficulties, used his passion for gardening to earn his livelihood, was responsible for the exquisite arrangement of the gardens. He planned them with knowledgeable foresight to create the lovely vistas seen from the house as the lawns sweep gently down to the lake formed by the damming of the River Wye. Look at it carefully and you will see it is in the shape of a swan. In this curving lake is an island reached by little stone bridges, and on it, beautifully positioned in its sylvan setting, is the Temple of Music.

High above it all the golden ball, topping the church upon the hill, is the focal point of the northern aspect. Made of copper beneath the gold it gleams in the sun and a ladder (now removed) gave access to the ball in which several people could sit. I have seen the number stated variously between six and twelve. Well, people do vary in size!

To the south of the Palladian dwelling, which I suppose is strictly the back, though its gracious portico and painted ceiling are far too sumptuous to be so designated, the gardens are separated from the cornfields beyond by a deep ha-ha, first dug out 200 years ago to prevent the deer in the park from wandering into the ornamental gardens. A ha-ha, or sunken fence, which has the advantage of dividing a garden from grazing or park land without impeding the view, was a French idea first used in England in 1712. Its French origin explains its name—the purely ejaculatory French *haha!*—stop!

29

12. *South Front, Wycombe Park*

The inside of the house is too lavish to describe here in any detail and the magnificent mahogany staircase inlaid with satin-wood rising up through a wide well is but one of its countless treasures. The hall is not only marble-floored but has marble walls as well. And, such are the vagaries of taste and fashion, that when the present owners came into residence these walls were covered by a coat of brown varnish and the original marble surface was only re-discovered quite accidentally. Other rooms contain Flemish tapestries older than the house; decorated ceilings, one depicting the marriage of Ariadne, another a Council of the Gods, and pictures, which if of mediocre quality, are of interest for the people they portray—Cromwell, Benjamin Franklin who paid several visits to the house, one of Milton's descendants who married a Dashwood, and Sir Francis himself.

Despite the well-planned motorway looping its way around the Wycombes a continuous flow of traffic still cuts through the main street of the village. But a few feet of pavement lie between its narrow length and the unbroken line of dwellings. The one of primary interest is generally accepted to be the Church Loft, of 1417, once a place of rest and refreshment for those who journeyed this way on the Oxford or

London roads. The over-hanging upper floor, little bell-turret, and clock on a metal bracket hanging out so that people may see the dial on either side, make it a picturesque sight. Glancing up I noted how the modern street lights were, in keeping with the clock, also suspended on metal brackets. The present clock is a little over 100 years old, but reference is made to one as far back as 1660. One heavy door is about a foot above pavement level, and there are five doors altogether indicating that at one time it was divided and let off as tenements. It is known that in the year 1845 Elizabeth Franklin was paying 3d. a week for a room at the back. The day I was last there drab curtaining masking the lower windows detracted from the idea that this was an historic part of our heritage being carefully preserved.

That West Wycombe was always a busy thoroughfare and coaching station is confirmed by its numerous inns. Three inn signs hang over the road; a triumphant St. George with his slain Dragon, the familiar Plough and a Swan. Two of these, the Swan and the George, appear on a map of 1767 which also names six more—the Wheel, Chequer, White Hart, Coach and Horses, Lion, and the Unicorn.

Dovecotes are glimpsed through the carriageway beside the George, and the one adjoining the Church Loft leads to Church Lane, a quiet, steep by-way running between pretty houses and a small furniture workshop, where the craftsmen's tools may be seen in the window. One house has an old pump outside, another the date 1722 over the porch and the house next to it has retained two fire insurance signs upon its walls. At the top a grass bank strategically situated between Fern Cottage and the Victorian school, allows a view of the weathered roof-tops angled into a haphazard design, and the village is revealed as a more complete whole than from any other viewpoint. Away from the street where the ancient houses are having a losing battle with the dirt and grime churned up by the cars, West Wycombe is seen as curiously untouched by time, and worthy of all the efforts made to preserve it.

Nevertheless, visitors have a definite choice, for the village is acknowledged as a honeypot area, attracting a constant flow of sight-seers. Go in summer, mix with the crowds, the children having rides upon the rare skewbald donkeys, and find the tourist-aimed exhibitions open. Or pay an out-of-season visit when, though unable to enjoy the contemporary attractions, you will see the village in comfort and can let your own imagination take over.

The A 40, having left the Wycombes, makes a gradual climb, and by the time it reaches Stokenchurch passing farm lands and high chalk banks, is bridging one of the highest of the Chiltern spurs. Even with the road bisecting its unusually large common land the overall impression of Stokenchurch is of space. The green may have been cut in two, but every possible square inch of turf has been preserved. Odd scraps of green occur throughout the village, some railed, some not. This is a place of sawmills and timber merchants, for as in Wycombe chair-making has employed Stokenchurch men for several generations. In various corners of the village great stacks of wood lie in wait. They represent some of the vast quantities of timber to have come from the Chiltern forests. Daniel Defoe in his journey through Buckinghamshire in the 1720's expressed astonishment at the amount of beechwood which was cut and carted to London.

"The quantity of this, brought from hence, is almost incredible", he wrote and went on to comment on the uses to which Londoners put it— "for billet wood for the King's palaces, for the plate and flint glass houses and other such nice purposes".

In the 19th century summer-time brought Irish and Welsh horses to Stokenchurch to the annual horse fair upon the common. One disadvantage of its position was that the village was frequently short of water and it is said that in 1870 it cost less to buy beer than water. The presence of a gigantic radio tower as the A 40 meets the motorway, and increasing development to both east and west has left Stokenchurch with only the remnants of a village. But behind the houses facing on to the common is the tiny Royal Oak at a junction of five by-ways, and a small commercial company nearby still stands cheek by jowl with a beech copse.

Mercifully the two villages of Radnage and Bledlow, lying between Stokenchurch and the gap in the hills at which the Upper Icknield Way moves in to the Chilterns have been avoided by the major roads. Surrounded by arable and pastoral land they remain withdrawn and undisturbed by heavy traffic. No two villages could be more dissimilar than Stokenchurch and Radnage. Sheltered by the Chiltern heights Radnage is set amidst a series of bottoms and twisting lanes. History records it as being noted for the longevity of its inhabitants, and suggests that its name was originally Radenach, meaning "red oak".

Extraordinarily it is divided into quite separate groups of cottages, some dating from the 16th and 17th centuries. The first to be encountered from Stokenchurch is, by ancient tradition, called The City. A school, a pub, a Mission Church and modern houses line the City Road. Though visually it is the least exciting part of Radnage, a thick fringe of thatch hangs over one minute cottage, and holly hedges are everywhere, as are country sounds and sights. On my last visit a man passed by with a bale of straw upon his back, a kestrel landed on a post by the wayside and a string of young horsemen cantered slowly up the road.

Between The City and the church are Bennett End and Town End to be reached by lanes which, though clearly named, it is both possible and worthwhile to meander round several times if you are not consulting a map. There is the subtlest of distinctions in Radnage between a lane and a road. As the houses cease and holly takes over Town End Road gives way to Sprigs Holly Lane. There is Radnage Lane, Green Lane and Bowers Lane, but as the latter leads into The City what could it meet other than City Road! A lane, so Chambers Dictionary tells us, is an old English name for a narrow passage or road. Far more evocative, and indeed more exact, is a 13th century definition which says that a lane need be wide enough for a cask of wine to be rolled along it with a man on either side.

Bennett End is a picturesque corner. The inn, The Three Horseshoes, much restored, bears the date 1745; doves flutter about The Three Cottages and the black and white Bennett End Farm completes the picture. Everything seems to be in threes in Radnage, and the third group, known as Town End, is the nearest to the church; a little church that should not be missed, for it is not just one more ancient monument to be visited for its architectural and historical interest, its brasses or its flowery epitaphs.

From the very recent (1968) re-pointing of all the exterior walls to the

13. *The Three Horseshoes, Radnage*

enthusiastically compiled booklet for visitors it reflects a vigorous approach to the modern concept of a village community; immensely proud of its heritage, yet spiritedly adapting itself to contemporary ideas.

For 600 years the church has stood here, but even before that it is very probable that it was a place of worship. There is evidence that it was the burial ground of early Celtic tribes, and some time after A.D. 700 the Anglo-Saxons, converted to Christianity by St. Berinus, probably built a church. The present font, unadorned and roughly hewn from stone, is thought to be Saxon and is known to have been unearthed in an adjacent field.

There are fragmentary mediaeval murals which, meticulously restored by E. Clive Rouse, make me wish I were ten feet tall and could see them more clearly. Some mediaeval tiles were also recovered and it was decided that an original way of displaying them would be to set them into a window sill. This has been done, but unfortunately the sill is only partially covered as the best of the tiles were stolen before the work was completed. Conversely, Little Kimble is believed to have acquired its set of outstanding 13th century tiles now in the chancel floor, by their being "filched" from Chertsey.

14. *Radnage Church*

34

A brass mounted on the wall beside the lectern remembers William Este and his family of eight boys and five girls. Only men of substance could afford the cost of a brass engraving and in 1524 he was the wealthiest of the nineteen taxpayers in Radnage, four of whom were named Este. Another incident of the same period illustrates the strictness of the hierarchy which existed in a village in Tudor times. An account of a manorial court in 1549 relates the case of a villager, William Wheler, whose bees were misguided enough to swarm within the demesne of the lord of the manor. For this unfortunate trespass William Wheler was fined a total of 2s.

In the days of the Civil War troops came through Radnage causing considerable destruction, as elsewhere throughout the Chilterns. All the pre-Cromwellian church glass was shattered with the exception of the one surviving piece of vivid blue in the west window. Within the village further demolition possibly took place in and around the years of the Plague. A group of cottages once formed a crescent south of the church. Evidence of their existence comes, not from archaeological diggings, but from an aerial view of building outlines seen before the crops are fully grown. And in the 1970's the present policy of this church is that, in addition to its place as a house of worship, it should be regarded as a functional building which can be a centre for other creative activities, such as the art exhibition which is held there every year.

The admirably proportioned Georgian rectory, since 1962 a private house, and the church are close neighbours upon the hillside. The house is in retreat behind a dark screen of yew, but the church has an extensive pastoral view to the south. To the north Radnage Lane twists and turns its way up out of the valley passing the secluded Bowers End Farm until eventually, with a sense of anti-climax, it emerges from the hedgerows to meet the Chinnor Road. Here the wind blows across the high ridge where a long row of dwellings forms the village of Bledlow Ridge.

Continuing north and over the course of the Upper Icknield Way is the far older village of Bledlow—which acquired its name from the Anglo-Saxon, Bledelawe, the bloody field or hill. The reference is to a savage battle believed to have been fought here between the Saxons and the Danes. Splendidly situated on the edge of the hills, overlooking the Aylesbury Vale, its first charm is the outstanding group of timbered cottages near the church. For more than 300 years the patina of time has mellowed the herring-bone brickwork and darkened the aged timbers, and old thatch has been replaced by new. The villagers have lived and died and new people have come and gone again, and around them the gardens have flowered, the trees have grown imperceptibly over the years.

15. *The Lions, Bledlow*

Now they are cherished and cared for, more, possibly, than ever before.

Bledlow is a place of changing mood and changing scene. From the triangular apron of green before the 17th century inn—oddly named The Lions and once three shepherds' cottages—the misty Vale below will vanish from sight if rain and cloud sweep across the sky. A south-westerly wind may effect a sudden transformation; within minutes the plains extending over the horizon to Thame and Oxford will re-appear, and it is a view to which distance does lend enchantment as even the smoking chimneys of Chinnor, though they cannot be denied, are less obvious from this height.

Behind the village and rising even higher to be 588 ft. above sea level, is Wain Hill. Marking the end of the Bledlow Ridge it has cut into its solid chalk the 15 ft. wide Bledlow Cross. The origin of Bledlow's White Cross and of the slightly larger Whiteleaf Cross overlooking the Risboroughs, remains an enigma. Maybe they were first cut out of the turf in the middle ages; alternatively other historians believe that they go back no further than the 17th century.

On The Cop, that is the northern slopes of Wain Hill, diggings of 1938 revealed finds dating from the Bronze Age to the Saxon period. Below the hill and across the railway line there lies evidence of Roman habitation and more than 600 years after the last Roman had left Britain, the Normans arrived in Bledlow and built a church beside a deep ravine. Pausing in the churchyard, by a row of hornbeams, where it drops dramatically down into a great chasm, I looked at the watercress beds far below in the River Lyde and could well understand why a bygone versifier was moved to say:

"They that live and do abide
Shall see the church fall into the Lyde."

The church, having survived so melodramatic a happening for nigh on 800 years, flaunts a blue-faced clock upon its grey flint exterior. Once through the massive Norman door there are impressive arcades and an Aylesbury type font the Normans made and used. Alterations have come gradually· throughout the centuries; there has been no major structural undertaking due to destruction by troops as at Radnage, or to the Victorian restoration fever. Searching around one or two curiosities come to light. Now relegated to a window sill is an 18th century wooden candle with a sham flame which once stood upon the altar, the only one of its kind I have ever seen. Above the south doorway is a mural of Adam and Eve, and the head of the traditional eagle on the lectern is turned round as if to keep his watchful eye upon the reader.

The road, staying in line with the Icknield Way, moves east out of the village to cross the end of the Wycombe Valley going below the railway line and on to meet the A 4010 which has made its way along the other side of the valley. Turning off the Wycombe Road by the rose-covered wall of the Red Lion to be, at once, in Bradenham, is rather like the raising of a curtain on a stage set.

Bradenham House and the church command the gradual slopes of a large rectangular green edged by stone boulders. Alongside, cottages are grouped into twos and threes. On closer inspection one turns out to be the village post office. The individual gardens and small orchards border the road to create a neat, stylised pattern against the backcloth of Bradenham Woods. Rarely is a village presented to you so completely, so unexpectedly as Bradenham from this approach. It is quite simply, as its Anglo-Saxon name proclaims, a "Brad", or broad, "Hamm", or village.

In 1086 it was unusually two Saxons, Suating and Herding, "who held Bradenham of the King". Nearly 500 years afterwards, in 1566, Bradenham was to see the pageantry of a royal procession when Queen Elizabeth I was entertained at the manor.

"Her Majesty and suite left Bradenham House on horseback, passing through some of the loveliest bits of primeval forest at Walter's Ashe, down Downley Common, through Tinker's Wood," and so she travelled on to Wycombe.

But it was when the Tudor and Stuart dynasties had given way to the house of Hanover that Bradenham gained by adoption a man who, in

37

common with so many Chiltern men, had no fear of abiding by his own belief however opposed to those of his fellows. In the year 1829 Isaac d'Israeli chose to move his family and his library of rare books from their London home to enjoy the country air of Buckinghamshire. Isaac was already sixty-six and in his own quiet way a rebel. He broke away from the Jewish faith of his ancestors and chose to have his children baptised in the Anglican Church. One of these children was to become a powerful statesman, a novelist and eventually Prime Minister and favoured friend of the Queen. Again contrary to what was expected of him he had chosen not to follow his father into business, but instead had turned to the study of literature.

Bradenham House became the d'Israelis' home, probably looking out-wardly little changed from how it does to-day. Dignified, substantial, with wrought-iron gates segregating it from the green it is set in gardens which are unashamedly formal; and at present is occupied by a computer firm. Ivy has crept along the mellow wall which grows high enough to be buttressed as it continues around the back of the gardens. The contrasting shapes of a yew, a larch and a Scots fir frame the gateway and the diversity of the trees, oak, ash, elm, beech as well as the evergreens, are one of the notable features of the village.

Once a stranger coming to Bradenham was so delighted by what he saw that he gave to the church a stone figure of St. Botolph, the patron saint, in appreciation of his much enjoyed visit. Bradenham is also the owner of two of the oldest church bells in England for they bear the inscription "Michael de Vvymbris me fecit", and Wymbish was casting bells when Edward I was on the throne.

I had quite a search before I discovered any acknowledgment of the d'Israelis. Eventually in the dim light of the vestry I did find a plain memorial plaque in remembrance of Isaac d'Israeli "author of 'Curiosities of Literature'," the book to which he devoted much of his life.

To the south-east of the village is Naphill Common and a wide stretch of deciduous woodland where inviting footpaths travel hither and thither. Ignoring these footpaths for the moment we will follow in Benjamin Disraeli's footsteps by travelling down into the Hughenden Valley and along Valley Road to the home he acquired for himself and his wife at Hughenden Manor in 1848. Here he spent the next thirty-three years of his life until he died.

The preservation of his home and 189 acres of estate by the National Trust is a fitting tribute to a man who lived life to the full, made a permanent mark in English history and never lost his genuine love of the Chiltern countryside. He inherited his father's passion for books, but his second

16. *Hughendon House*

passion was for trees. Both could be contemplated in silence. The massive cedar of Lebanon at the far end of the terraces at Hughenden is 122 years old having been planted by Disraeli himself. Although fond of the beeches, he had a particular liking for conifers. Wherever he looked at Hughenden trees were part of the landscape as they still are.

In the gardens statues, Grecian ladies, Pan-like figures and a comic pair of dwarfs enliven the terraces. Peacocks no longer strut between them. Visitors amble slowly round with cameras poised in these gardens of which Disraeli wrote with delight:

"We have made a garden of terraces in which cavaliers might roam and saunter with their ladye-loves."

The gardener at Hughenden, who takes an immense pride in his work, told me emphatically that the grounds are at their best in early spring when the daffodils and crocus are in flower. He pointed out the two sun-dials. One is upon the terraces, but the second, less detailed and far older dial is attached to a corner of the stables and bears the date 1749. Owing to the height and size of the opposite trees I think the summer sun rarely reaches it.

Numerous tales are told of the eccentricities of Disraeli. He was renowned for his love of making an effect. As a young man he had a fondness for gaily coloured waistcoats, and even after his entry into politics was to be seen in a Tyrolean hat, or some similar striking dress. The solid house he bought at Hughenden after his marriage to Mary

39

17. *Sundial on Corner of Stables, Hughendon*

Anne Wyndham Lewis in 1839 was to receive many adornments. The architect, E. B. Lamb, was commissioned to add certain "dramatic improvements". Architectural purists have made derisive comments about Hughenden, but it is as Disraeli wished it to be re-fashioned and he was very happy here.

I have a liking for the ornamental groups of chimneys. They resemble statues silhouetted against the sky, and a television aerial appears to be held above the heavy gabling by a row of archbishops. Every afternoon, except Mondays and all through January, part of the house is open to the public as a Disraeli museum. The Gothic dining room is where Queen Victoria lunched with her Prime Minister in December 1877. In other rooms are to be found the desk at which he wrote, his books, notes from the Queen, the primroses she sent to him, faded and pressed, the manuscript of his novel "Coningsby", a chair made especially for him in High Wycombe, and another, once the property of Edmund Burke. All are displayed in rooms amply provided with embroidered chairs and footstools, gilt-edged furniture, screens, rich dark wallpaper and a wealth of reminiscent Victoriana.

Below the manor, and carefully folded into the southern slope of the hillside is the church where Disraeli, by his own request, lies at rest. In the chancel is a simple memorial plaque inscribed:

"To the dear and honoured memory of Benjamin Disraeli, Earl of Beaconsfield, this memorial is placed by his grateful and affectionate sovereign and friend, Victoria R.I."

A step or two south-west of the church is a group of almshouses built on the estate during the 17th century by the Dormer family to whom the manor was granted after the dissolution of the monasteries. Gabled, with mullioned windows they are a good example of the attractiveness of many almshouses throughout the Chilterns.

18. *Benjamin Disraeli, 1st Earl of Beaconsfield*

An extra pleasure of Hughenden is the pattern of footpaths threading their way through the woodland beyond the house. It was here that I met a man from Downley who told me how he used to see a pair of badgers on his way home "from the penny-pictures at Wycombe". They kept the foxes away, he said. Whilst the badger sett was inhabited a fox was never seen in the neighbourhood. One day a foolish young man shot the female, the male disappeared, and the very next night a fox raided the chicken run.

Risborough to Hampden

CHAPTER III

The stage at which a village develops into a small town is not always easy to define. So in writing of villages of the Chilterns I have allowed myself a certain licence to include one or two of outsize proportions.

Prince's Risborough, an ancient demesne of the Black Prince who is said to have had a palace here, is such a place. In spite of its strategic position athwart the junction of the Icknield Way and the valley road from Wycombe to the Vale, it has not lost the air of a quiet, market town. During the 17th century the portrait painter, Sir Peter Lely, had a farm in the district. His portrait of Sir William Penn, father of the Quaker from nearby Hampden, is in the Gallery of Greenwich Hospital. In 1861 the town had numerous parchment-maker's and woolstapler's yards as well as two breweries and three malt-houses. Thursdays brought the farmers to Risborough for the corn and cattle market.

Conveniently the ideal landmark from which to begin an exploration of the older quarter is the car park beside the Church of St. Mary. One of the few Chiltern spires rises up from the chequered parapet of the tower; a tower that caused Risborough considerable trouble at the turn of the 19th century. A few entries from the Churchwardens' accounts tell their own tale:

1804	Feb.	1st	The Church Tower fell down			
		4th	4 men 4 days removing the rubbish	1	4	0
		11th	Sundry labourers ditto	1	10	3
		and	Mr. Grace for buying articles stolen from the church			6
	Aug.	24th	Journey to London to sell the Bells	2	0	0
	Sept.	6th	Beer on removing the Bells		3	9
		22nd	Postage on several letters respecting the Bells		5	3
1805	June	25th	Jas. Bampton carre of small bell from London		2	6
1806	May	13th	Paid Thomas Lacey (for repair work)	60	0	0

19. Church Tower, Princes Risborough

The six bells, damaged as tower and spire collapsed, were sold to a firm in Whitechapel to raise funds to cope with the emergency. Unfortunately the overall repair was apparently unsatisfactory, and in 1908, John Oldrid Scott, the architect son of the more famous Gilbert Scott, was commissioned to restore both tower and spire.

Some good old houses are collected in the triangle formed by church, Manor House and Market Hall. No doubt they are some of those which the historian Sheahan called "very genteel". Several being no longer privately owned we may have the pleasure of seeing inside. The town library, in a much restored timber-framed building, has a wealth of

20. Vine House, Princes Risborough

exceedingly picturesque beams. Across the street the Tudor Vine House displays antiques in its windows, but the once magnificent vine is a shadow of its former self. The Market Hall, erected in 1824, is the central feature of the square. One side serves as a bus shelter, but when Risborough enjoys the usual bustle of a Saturday morning, watercress, sprouts, cauliflowers, cucumbers (some I saw marked curiously "large half") and seasonal fruits pack the stalls tightly wedged between the wooden posts.

The Manor House, formerly Brook House, is of red brick, dated 1670 and renowned for its superb Jacobean staircase. Presented to the National Trust in 1925 by the widow of Charles Rothschild, it is open to the public on Tuesday and Wednesday afternoons. Further along the lane is the Old Vicarage, a gem of the 15th century. Irregular projections, quaint windows and a hefty chimney-stack enclosing an ingle-nook, all contribute in creating a house straight out of Hans Andersen. From 1937 to '38 it was the home of Amy Johnson, who as a pioneer of women aviators captured the imagination of the public.

Facing this intriguing cottage, which is still privately owned, are a group of old barns standing round three sides of a farmyard. The cow-sheds and stables stand empty with doors ajar; grass is establishing itself quickly over the yard, and the fate of the Manor Farm lies in the balance.

Whether some of the barns, for they are rather splendid ones, may be preserved and what might take their place is being argued out between planners and conservationists.

The lesser of the two Risboroughs belonged until Henry VIII's appropriation of ecclesiastical lands, to the Monks of Christ Church, Canterbury. Frequently it loses its suffix to be familiarly called "Monks". Although new development is in progress all around as the houses of Risborough fan out to join it the centre of Monks has maintained its reputation as a haven of sequestered calm. It would be very easy to hurry along the A 4010 from Risborough and miss Mill Lane as it turns off by the War Memorial to meet Burton Lane and a group of the most prepossessing cottages it would be possible to find anywhere. Walnut trees shade the pocket-sized low-walled gardens. Thatch, weathered timbers and brick all play their part. I found a pattern of herring-bone brick, the date 1590 upon a porch, and a single piece of carved stonework set into a brick face.

Or ignoring the particular, it is a place in which to linger and having absorbed its serenity wander along the alleyway to discover the friendly church of St. Dunstan. A church to which ever since the 14th century craftsmen have applied their skills in stone, in wood, and in brass. There

21. *Cottages, Monks Risborough*

46

are Perpendicular windows, carved figures on the bench ends and a two-foot brass of Robert Blundell, a former rector, as well as an un-named family group. Beside the church a gateway leads to a field where children play on brightly painted swings and slides. A few steps from their play-ground is a square building, not very big and made of stone. Like windmills and smithys, mediaeval dovecotes are one of the vanishing sights of the English countryside, and the box-like design of the one at Monks, though of the more ordinary type, has survived since the 16th century. The recesses for the doves can be seen at the back; there is a miniature lantern, or turret, on top and an odd Gothic door believed to have been added later.

Built when only the clergy or the lord of the manor were allowed to keep doves, it does suggest that there may have been a monastery (though there is little evidence of this) or a manorial house here at some period. Dovecotes were then simply a question of domestic economy—young pigeon was good to eat particularly when winter brought a shortage of meat. More picturesque examples are the octagonal dovecote at Stewkley, and the circular type to be seen at Hurley in Berkshire.

Almost equidistant from Risborough are the outlying hamlets of White-leaf, sheltered in the lee of the hill, and Askett tucked in between the foot-hills and the plains. An air of quiet seclusion surrounds the older cottages of Whiteleaf gathered along the course of the Upper Icknield Way. Although the Red Lion does hang out a "No Hikers" sign, which, as an advocate of walking, I found rather off-putting, everyone else I met at Whiteleaf was exceptionally friendly. I learnt much about the village from amiable conversation.

Barn Cottage was, but is no longer, the village store, selling anything and everything. Charcoal burners, active in the woods in earlier days, once lived in the 400 year old cottages now converted and modernised. Whiteleaf, in common with most other Chiltern villages, fights hard to restrict new development, but does not always succeed. It looks with dismay at the over-bright red brick of the "quality" houses, and regrets the Paddock which was there before. The inhabitants are aware of the housing problem and realise they are fortunate, but they realise also that it rests with them to try and preserve their own especial corner of the environment, not only for themselves but for those who come afterwards.

In Askett at the wide meeting place of Letter Box, Askett and Pound Lanes I was fortunate enough to find the thatch upon the long, low and very pretty Askett Farm Cottage in the process of being renewed. Origin-ally "thatch" meant just any roof or cover, but gradually changed to specify the material, either straw, reed or sedge, used for what was the

22. *Thatching at Askett*

cheapest, most common and warmest type of roofing. In the reign of Edward III a thatcher was paid 2d. or 3d. a day, whilst the yelmer, who collected the reeds into yelms, or bundles, ready for the thatcher to use, earned only 1d. Devon-straw thatch is reckoned to last about 20 years, and now, I was told, "Norfolk reed costs more, but it'll last a good 50 or 60—if you can get it."

Pound Lane leaves Askett to cross the railway and join the B 4009. From this straight run of the Lower Icknield Way the true significance of the western escarpment is well realised. The Chiltern Hills rise up from the level Vale to curve across the eastern horizon, and seen from afar, even these unpretentious heights preserve an air of mystery about their thickly wooded slopes.

On Whiteleaf Hill is the Greek Cross cut 80 foot across into the chalk, and with arms some 20 foot wide. Further north on Beacon Hill are the earthworks of the fortress built by Cunobelinus, King of the Britons in the 1st century A.D. From this encampment he and his men are thought to have resisted the Romans. And on Coombe Hill, accepted at 852 feet as the highest point of the Chilterns, the memorial to the men who lost their lives in the South African Wars of 1899–1902 is outlined against the sky.

23. *Monument on Coombe Hill, highest point of Chilterns*

As well as holding evidence of an earlier civilisation the line of hills are of botanical interest for the growth of box upon the Kimble–Ellesborough escarpment. About 200 years ago box covered an area of 150 acres, and not only was it noted for giving cover to innumerable rabbits, but was also used readily as firewood by the people of Kimble. To-day it is valued as too precious to be cut at all, for apart from Box Hill in Surrey, it is one of the few districts in England where it is found growing wild.

No one can pass Great Kimble's church raised on its individual mound, without recalling that it was here that John Hampden, the Patriot, recorded with his fellow protesters, their refusal to pay King Charles' ship-money levy. Because the busy A 4010 runs through contemporary Kimble it is wiser to take to the footpaths. Beyond the church is Manor Farm and a little brook, one of several springing up out of the chalk between Risborough and Wendover, flows from a pool beside the tall elms. To the east of the road a bridleway near Cymbeline's Cottage climbs steeply up Pulpit (formery Bulpit) Hill. It is characteristic of many Chiltern tracks. Bramble, hawthorn and hedgerow trees linked by the twining stems of traveller's joy give protection from wind, rain and sun. In the densely packed banks are old rabbit warrens; red spikes of cuckoo-pint and green spurge shoot up through the brushwood. There is little sound except the call of a wren darting from bush to bush, the scuffle of a blackbird in the leaves, or the sweet notes of a summer warbler. Beyond Kimble's shaded track there are poppies and forget-me-nots in the cornfields, wild rose in the hedgerows and sturdy woodruff beneath the beeches. White bedstraw is its country name and when dried and placed in the linen cupboard its delicate scent will last longer than lavender.

Only a quarter of a mile divides the two Kimble churches, and just over half a mile north-east of Little Kimble is Ellesborough, a prominent

24. *Cymbeline's Cottage, Great Kimble*

landmark high above the road. All three churches were founded in the 13th and 14th centuries but whilst the bold flint exterior of St. Nicholas at Little Kimble, and St. Peter and St. Paul at Ellesborough are Victorian-restored, the infinitely smaller and admirably proportioned building at Little Kimble is essentially a mediaeval church.

In the middle ages an unknown artist used his imagination, knowledge and undoubted skill to create a series of murals at Little Kimble; pictures used as a visual aid by the rector in the instruction of his parishioners. March 1972 saw the commencement of restoration work on the sadly fading figures. Traces of eleven saints have been identified, and I saw St. Bernard clad in a flowing robe, and St. George, a simple portrayal with neither horse nor dragon. The chancel floor contains the Chertsey tiles already mentioned. Each four tiles constitutes a roundel, their worn surfaces depicting characters from the Arthurian legend.

The *Victoria County History* refers to the church in 1839 as being "sufficient to accommodate inhabitants" and the village is still no more than a scattered collection of houses and farms. As at Kimble there is water, and the Bonny Brook gushes out quite vigorously alongside the churchyard.

Ellesborough claims a special place in both the history of the Chilterns,

25. *Little Kimble Church*

and of the country as a whole. With Chequers close at hand its fame rests in its associations, and General de Gaulle and General Eisenhower are but two of the distinguished men who have joined the congregation of St. Peter and St. Paul.

In 1917, with a truly benevolent gesture and an idyllic belief in the restorative qualities of the pure country air, Lord Lee of Fareham gave Chequers to the nation. One of the stipulations made by Lee was that the name, Chequers, should not be changed. Mr. J. Gilbert Jenkins in his authoritative book says that it is derived from Elias Hostiarius, an usher of the Exchequer in the 13th century who was granted some land in Ellesborough. The exact origins of the house are not known, but it was probably rebuilt in the 1560's by William Hawtrey, one of the wealthiest landowners of the district.

When the twenty-five year old Lady Mary Grey, sister of Lady Jane, was in disgrace for having married the Sergeant-Porter, Thomas Keys, in secret, she was despatched to Chequers to be under Hawtrey's guardianship. Poor Lady Mary who had crept out one August evening, and at a candlelit marriage service had become the wife of Keys, so much below

26. *Gateway to Chequers*

51

her in rank, and towering above her in stature. Queen Elizabeth never forgave her, and Keys was only freed after three years imprisonment on the condition he never saw his wife again.

The letting of the house to Arthur Lee was the first step towards it becoming the country retreat of the leaders of the Government. Henry Jacob Astley, the owner at that time, distinguished himself as one of the earliest aviators and lost his life in 1912 during a flying demonstration, giving Lee the opportunity of buying Chequers. He and his rich American wife loved their home and did a great deal to improve and restore it to its Elizabethan state.

David Lloyd George was the first Prime Minister to occupy the house. He began the custom of the Minister's memorial trees by adding an oak to the fine trees of the 1,232 acre estate. The main drive, The Victory Way, is lined by a row of young beech, the gift of Winston Churchill. Ministers come and go, the trees remain.

From the lodge gates of Chequers the road makes a well defined double loop, passes the motorist's stop for Coombe Hill and the Monument, narrows as it climbs through High Scrub and Fugsden Wood to arrive at Dunsmore. The houses of Dunsmore huddle together as if for companionship and security, and the names upon the gates, Outlook, Tree-tops, Moonrising are indicative of their position perched 700 foot up on a hill-top. Two inns, The Black Horse and The Fox, serve this hamlet and beyond them the roads peter out to be replaced by footpaths. Farmyard ducks swim on the pond; sociable ducks moving eagerly towards the bank on the look-out for food. Village ponds are a rare feature of the sparsely watered Chilterns. Writing of another place William Allingham expressed their universal appeal:

> "Four ducks on a pond,
> A grass bank beyond,
> A blue sky of spring,
> White clouds on the wing,
> What a little thing
> To remember for years."

27. *Signpost, Dunsmore*

28. *Topiary at Smalldean Farm, Wendover*

The looping road does not end in Dunsmore, but leaves the hill, encounters Smalldean Farm made impressive by its black timbered barns (one is converted to a studio) and ornate topiary, and eventually meets the Wendover Road.

There is much to see in Wendover. Its ancient connections begin with the main thoroughfare, Rupert Brooke's "Roman road to Wendover", travelling from Ellesborough and on to Tring at the northern end of the town. Domesday names it as Waendofron, derived from an old English name meaning "white water", i.e. water running through chalk. The accurate derivation was a disappointment to me; I had previously enjoyed a simple picture of Chaucerian-type travellers wending their way across the neighbouring hills.

The town's manorial owners make impressive, and lengthy, reading. In the 16th century lands in Wendover changed ownership more often than Henry VIII changed wives. Lands which the King had given to Catherine of Aragon passed to Jane Seymour and then to Anne of Cleves and Catherine Howard, after which they reverted to the Crown. Elizabeth gave them to Sir Francis Knollys in 1564 and within the next ten years they were sold to William Hawtrey of Chequers. For a further long period Wendover was controlled by the Hampdens. Although one of the smallest boroughs in England it had, between 1625 and 1832, the privilege of sending two burgesses to Parliament and was at different times represented by Hampden, Richard Steele, founder of The Tatler and man of letters, Burke and Canning.

29. *Aylesbury Road, Wendover*

Roger of Wendover, a chronicler of St. Albans in the reign of Henry III, wrote one of the earliest of our history books, "Flowers of History". Of the same period is Richard of Wendover who became Bishop of Rochester and was held in high esteem by the King.

The old and the new are harmoniously combined in Wendover. New shops, such as the King's Head Parade and the contemporary library do not intrude upon the antiquity of the "praty thoroughfare". The Two Brewers is at least 300 years old, Robert Louis Stevenson and possibly Cromwell, stayed at the Red Lion, Vine Tree Farm in Back Street is of the 18th century and at the foot of the hill the Clock Tower was presented to the town by Abel Smith in 1842. The lower part was once the lock-up. From a plaque at the back I learnt that the clock is the "Property of ye parish by contributions from the Vicar, Landowners and Occupiers". There is the Georgian elegance of Lime Tree House in Pound Lane, and the post office is in the 16th century Bosworth House. In the 1920's it made news when, during alterations, murals as old as the house were discovered. They were divided between the Victoria and Albert and Aylesbury museums. Just through the carriage-way alongside a piscina, or basin in which vessels used at Mass were washed, is set into the wall.

54

Its presence there is not precisely explained, though suggestions have been made that the house might be of monastic origin.

Wendover's 14th century church is isolated from the town, and owes much to its rural setting. Sycamores and limes take their place amongst the orthodox yews. It is reached by a quarter of a mile of pathway, shaded by beech and elm and following the course of a crystal-clear stream.

Trees are an integral part of the town. A group of Scots pine top the Clock Tower. A chestnut adds its splendour to the centre of the High Street. And in the two foot gap by Pear Tree Cottage, a pear tree does still grow, bravely displaying its white blossom above the low roof of the neighbouring Bank.

Tring Road is redeemed from mediocrity by Bank Farm, one of the oldest existing buildings in Wendover, and the eleven Coldharbour Cottages. This outstandingly picturesque row, with tiny windows peering out below deep thatch, have origins going back to 1600. Around the corner the wide Aylesbury Road is noted for its unbroken line of gracious 18th century houses. Once from their windows it was possible to see the turning sails of Wendover's octagonal mill. But although its active life outlived that of Cobstone Mill at Turville, its sails, damaged by a storm, were removed in 1904. A steam engine was installed and operated until 1926, and the mill is now a private residence.

30. *Coldharbour Cottages, Wendover*

31. Hampden House, Great Hampden

In 1972 Wendover added to its history by producing, under the editorship of the town librarian, Richard Snow, "The New History of Wendover" which was "a joint effort by the whole Wendover community".

In all the Buckinghamshire Chilterns no place is as remote as Little Hampden, three miles south of Wendover. The Buckinghamshire writer J. H. B. Peel calls it a "still and secluded hamlet". The road past the blacksmith's, signposted "To Little Hampden only", seems to wind unendingly on. Only when it meets the Common and the Rising Sun does it finally come to a full stop. Manor Farm is here with its good, weatherboarded barns. Since the Normans came there has been a church. Inside no less than four murals of St. Christopher, three on the north wall, two being superimposed, and one on the south wall, have been very recently discovered.

Little Hampden is a place in which to pause and take a stroll on the Common where birch, elder and thorn grow above the bracken. In summer it is bright with the yellow St. John's Wort, pink loosestrife and the hard-heads of purple knapweed.

Associations with the Patriot, John Hampden, are to be found throughout the Chilterns; but Great Hampden, where he spent his childhood,

56

seems the appropriate place in which to recall the well known facts of his history. Born in 1595, the eldest son of William Hampden, a wealthy Buckinghamshire squire, he was, on his mother's side, a first cousin of Oliver Cromwell. He must have made countless journeys across the western borders of the hills, and on over the expansive Aylesbury Plain, for he was educated at the Grammar School in Thame and was later a student at Magdalen College, Oxford. At the age of twenty-four he married Elizabeth Symeon of Pyrton in Oxfordshire. He brought his charming wife to Hampden House, and she bore him nine children.

His roots, his home and his beloved family were in Great Hampden, but it was at Great Kimble in January 1635, only a few months after the death of Elizabeth, that the simple and historic document was drafted which established Hampden's name as for ever synonymous with the freedom of the individual. The levy on his lands at Stoke Mandeville was 20s. but to pay it would have condoned the tyranny of the King.

He lived in troubled times. In 1642 Hampden drew together and commanded a regiment, The Green Coats. That Hampden's tenants and neighbours followed him out of loyalty and regard is undoubtedly true, but many of these sturdy Chiltern men were unfaltering in their belief in the justice of the fight for the Parliamentary cause. A cause for which Hampden was to give his life. On June 18th, 1643 the Cavaliers charged down through Stokenchurch to surprise and scatter the opposing troops in the small village of Chinnor. Making a cunning retreat after their successful attack they tempted the Roundheads under the command of Sir Philip Stapleton and Hampden to come after them. In the now famous cornfield at Chalgrove Hampden received a wound in the shoulder— six days later he died in Thame, and was buried at Great Hampden.

32. *Great Hampden Church*

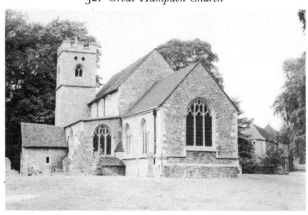

57

According to Pevsner, Hampden House has at least one detail, the inner doorway to King John's Tower at the south front, dating from the 14th century. The house has undergone considerable alteration and the Gothic battlements and decorative frieze were all added about 1750. One of the best preserved sections of Grim's Dyke runs through Hampden Park, and the tale is told that when Elizabeth I paid a visit to Griffith Hampden he levelled part of the Dyke to ensure her approach was as easy as possible.

A stretch of the parkland divides the church and house from Hampden Row. Hardly a village, it is just a handful of houses, The Hampden Arms and the green beside the beechwoods, the scene of many a cricket match.

When Ramsay MacDonald was Prime Minister, and living at Chequers in the 1920's, one of his favourite walks was over Coombe Hill and back through Great Hampden. Inevitably there have been changes. But Hampden is still partially enclosed by woodland and there are many miles of the Great Hampden estate through which to walk to Speen (where MacDonald's daughter, Ishbel, once ran the Plow) to the White-leaf Cross, or through to those lanes around the Pink and Lily at Parslow's Hillock where Rupert Brooke once roamed with Cathleen Nesbitt.

CHAPTER IV

Missenden to Hedgerley

With the coming of the metropolitan line, part of the Chilterns, Buckinghamshire in particular, became commuter country. One of the villages which expanded to accommodate the steadily increasing demand for a house in the country was Great Missenden. Change has taken place not only since the railway, but also between the 1950's and 1970's. Until the road (A 413) was built to by-pass it all traffic between Amersham and Wendover passed through Missenden's main street. So narrow is the High Street that any traffic at all tends to crowd it. Yet so direct is the thoroughfare that it might lead you on and out again without indication that should you care to stop there is more to see.

33. *The George, Great Missenden High Street*

Boutiques have joined the village shops; the Black Lion faces the White Lion, and a Bank occupies the site of the Buckinghamshire Arms. The ancient beams of the George are said to date back to 1480, and through an archway is the long, two-storeyed and timbered Court-House. Standing back in un-protestant fashion is the rather splendid Baptist Chapel. This large, stuccoed building was built in 1838 at a cost of £1,200. Dissenters were present in Missenden much earlier, and a small Meeting-House had been erected in 1776. Only demolished because it was unsafe, it was replaced by the present chapel.

Missenden was visited by John Leland when making his *"Laborious journey and search for England's Antiquities"*, the results of which he presented to Henry VIII as a New Year's Gift. He called the village "a quiet old-fashioned place, with no actual picturesque features, but reposeful with its unostentatious dwellings grouped below the beechwoods". Nevertheless, Missenden has always had a certain importance. In 1133 William de Missenden chose this situation as a suitable place for the founding of an Abbey of Augustinian Canons. The River Misbourne provided the first essential, water; the hills gave shelter, and the beechwoods fuel and a feeding ground for the pigs.

The Abbey had its ups and downs. The ways of the monks were devious and their reputation was not always of the highest. In the reign of Edward III one of them was hanged for clipping the coinage. Just

34. *Missenden Abbey, Great Missenden*

prior to the suppression, in 1531, Abbot Fox was accused of immorality and ordered to be suspended. Such punishments were not always enforced, and despite his misconduct he remained in office until his death. From time immemorial the scandalous makes news, and the names of those monks who led unblemished lives less frequently enter our history books.

The Dissolution sent the Abbey monks out into the world in common with others all over the country. Afterwards the Abbey changed hands quite often, and its various owners from the Fleetwoods who had purchased it from Robert, Earl of Leicester, to the Carringtons, who bought it in 1815, all had a hand in pulling down and refashioning the original building. In 1946 the Abbey, now in Gothic style, was sold to the Buckinghamshire County Council for use as an adult college.

Standing apart and above the town the Church of St. Peter and St. Paul is reached by a bridge over the by-pass. It offers an excellent viewpoint from which to appreciate Missenden's favourable position in the Misbourne Valley. Fine chestnut, oak and cedar grace the Abbey grounds, and sheep graze in the meadow. The A 413 below the bridge speeds on through open country to Wendover. Undisturbed hedgerows are still part of the surrounding agricultural pattern. Most suffer the chopping of a mechanical cutter, but occasionally the work of a craftsman is seen in a finely layered, or "eddered", hedgerow. At the end of the winter before the new foliage is sprouting, upright stakes are placed about 1½ foot apart. The branches of the existing hedge are partly cut near to the roots and then woven length-ways between the stakes. The finished hedge resembles basket work, and forms an impenetrable barrier.

The Misbourne rises at the northern end of the village, springing up in Mobwell meadow facing the Black Horse. There are years when it dries up completely and the pool, where children sometimes paddle, is just an empty grass hollow. Then only the bending willow suggests there might have been water here. Missenden sees little of the elusive Misbourne until it waters the Abbey grounds and makes its way to Little Missenden, interestingly referred to by Leland as "a strete a mile and a halfe lower further towards London than Great Missenden". A "strete" then meant a small place without a market.

Craftsmen of all ages have had a hand in the construction of the church of St. John the Baptist at Little Missenden. A line from the Vicar's notes says, "the porch is almost our most recent addition, and that in 1450". Briefly it was founded by the Anglo-Saxons, has Roman bricks in the chancel arch, and the Normans added the workmanlike nave arches. Upon the walls is the early mediaeval "Bible of the Poor". A sudden shaft of sunlight will illumine the indeterminate figures of the giant St.

35. "Eddered" hedge at Great Missenden

Christopher, his feet in the water, St. Catherine, and the angel with a scroll looking down on a shepherd boy playing his pipe.

Apart from the more obvious historic points of interest there are three items connected with the church of singular appeal. The first is a single stone step beneath the vestry door. Its uneven surface, trodden down by countless feet, bears witness to its age: being one of the original stones of the church, it is 1,000 years old. The second is a brass tablet on the wall of the Baptistry which ensures that a villager named Rebecca Saltonshall is never quite forgotten by extolling her virtues. But the dates of her birth and death carry a special significance: "Born December 1727, Old Style—died December 1758, New Style". During Rebecca's lifetime, in 1752, England adopted the Gregorian Calendar by which eleven days were omitted from the previous calendar. A decision which nearly brought the Government down as people protested "Give us back our eleven days". Finally since 1959 the church has been the main auditorium for Little Missenden's annual festival of music and the arts.

Overlooking the church grounds is the Jacobean Manor House; a house which, as its wall curves round with the road, is an intimate part of the village scene. Here lived Dr. Bates, intimate friend of the artist Angelica Kaufmann, doctor to Francis Dashwood of High Wycombe, and one of the oldest survivors of the Hell-Fire Club. He lived to be ninety-eight and to the end of his days repeated emphatically that the stories of

36. The Manor House, Little Missenden

Dashwood's doubtful activities were "scandalous and sarcastic fabrications".

Manor, church, Town Farm, post office and cottages are all closely assembled and the by-ways reach out north, south, east and west. Farm barns and hay-ricks are here right in the village; a weathervane on the Manor out-buildings depicts a huntsman with his hounds, and a pair of cottages stand at right angles to the lane allowing a picture of the open country beyond. Beyond the Red Lion, where the stagecoach used to call, and the Crown, where Toby's Lane climbs to Mop End, the Misbourne reappears. Having skirted the village, the little river flows under the road by the lovely 17th century Mill House. Meandering on through the water meadows to Amersham it hurries over the pebbles to attain its full beauty as it widens into Shardeloes Lake.

Instead of following the Misbourne to Amersham let us take the road to Penn. On the way the road passes the cruciform church at Penn Street restored by Earl Howe, its spire rising higher than the beech trees. From an inn, the Hit or Miss, swings an unusual sign. A game of cricket in its original form is in progress. Only two stumps form the wicket and the batsman wearing a tasselled cap and a yellow jerkin over his mauve leggings holds his bat on high. His bat resembles a curved hockey-stick (they did not become straight until about 1770) and his fellow-players,

63

equally gaily dressed, watch expectantly for his hit or miss. Cricket was first of all a countryman's game and one which in mediaeval days was actually forbidden by law in case it interfered with archery practice.

People come to Penn for the air, the church, the Crown Inn and the view; the order is strictly alphabetical. Spreading out across the top of the escarpment nearly 600 ft. above sea level Penn connects up with Tyler's Green as if they were one. The low walls, white fencing and colourful gardens of the small group of shops they share have the gratifying effect of resembling a village within a village. Pollarded elms line the green where, every September, the annual pleasure fair, allowed by Charter, still takes place. Like Dunsmore, this hill-top village has a pond, and opposite is the footpath to the oldest building in Penn, Puttenham Place, a farm which has stood for 500 years like an island amidst the fields.

It is said that from the tower of the 14th century church it is possible to see twelve counties. With no attempt at such a claim I do know that in the nearby lane, from the gateway opposite Paul's Hill Cottage, there are wide views as the hill ridges roll away south to the Thames Valley. Looking north from beside the 300-year old Crown, Vicarage Wood drops steeply to Penn Bottom, and the horizon is ringed by woodland.

37. *Street in Penn*

Accounts of the church in the middle ages are vague. The Bishop of Lincoln had a Palace at Wooburn, south of Penn, and men of the district suspected of Lollard sympathies were dispatched to the Palace dungeons. Names of men accused by Longland as heretics, Dean, Dell, Harding, Hobbes, Nash are still to be found in the locality.

Sybil Hampden, nurse and governess to the delicate boy Edward VI at Ashridge, was given the living of Holy Trinity, Penn, on the occasion of her marriage to David Penn. Sybil died of small-pox in 1562. Her husband survived her and the especial significance of timber in those days is shown in his bequest to a servant, Anne Playter, and her husband of ten beech trees.

The last Penn of Penn House was Roger Penn who died intestate in 1731. He was unmarried, as were his three brothers and four of his sisters. The estate passed to the eldest sister, Sarah, wife of Sir Nathaniel Curzon. Penn House now belongs to Earl Howe who is descended from Sarah Penn.

William Penn (1644–1718) Quaker and founder of Pennsylvania, believed he was related to the Penns of Penn, though there has never been any factual evidence to support his claim. But there is no doubt that he knew and had an affection for the village, and a stone marks the burial place of his grandsons, the children of Thomas Penn.

A church is rather like a home to which a family brings back its treasures. At Penn the pulpit with its marquetry panels was a gift of the Curzons from a Mayfair Chapel. A heavy chest is ornately carved, and people have scratched their initials on the smooth surface of the simple leaden font as they do on the bark of a beech. Of the fine array of Penn brasses, the most striking group is of John Penn, who died in 1597, his wife and their five sons and daughters who are engraved quite charmingly to show their varying ages. Investigations on the roof in 1938 brought to light a Doom painting of the late 15th century. So highly placed is it above the chancel arch that it is not easy to see it very clearly, but the figures of Christ and the angels, in rich shades of red and orange, are painted on board. This makes it a rarity, as there are only three similar paintings in the country. Distinguished by having only one hand, the clock on the tower was repaired after a lengthy silence and "set going Easter 1925 through the unaided efforts of Patricia Cuthbert aged 13".

Writers and musicians known the world over have stayed and lived in Penn. In 1796 Edmund Burke used a house in a field, since called French School Meadow, as a school for fatherless French children. In the garden of Penn House Handel is said to have composed part of the *Messiah*. Arthur Sullivan came to Watercroft to stay with Sir George Grove, and in

1898–9 the French novelist Emile Zola sought retreat at Penn after championing the Dreyfus case. In contemporary times the lyric poet Walter de la Mare travelled here from his Twickenham home to stay with his daughter.

A celebrated native of Penn was Jack Shrimpton. Born in 1671, the son of a respected villager, he became known as a daring and persistent highwayman. His greatest haul was the robbery of three or four coaches near Gerrard's Cross when he took £150 from the passengers. After countless escapades he was arrested in Bristol for drunken behaviour. He shot the watchman who was escorting him, a final crime which cost him his life.

At the western tip of the village where the War Memorial and a huge hollow elm share a triangle of green, the road continues by Penbury Farm—William Penn is thought to have remembered it when he called his Pennsylvania home "Pennsbury"—and through the prosperous modernity of Knotty Green to Beaconsfield.

History speaks from every corner of Beaconsfield. The new town has developed in the vicinity of the station, but the spacious old town has kept its separate personality. It grew up at the cross-roads of the coaching

38. *The White Hart, Beaconsfield*

routes to Windsor and Oxford. Coaches journeyed through wild and wooded country so beset by highwaymen, such as Jack Shrimpton, that the local saying, "Here, if you beat a bush 'tis odds you'd start a thief" was almost literally true.

As he approached the town the guard would blow his long horn to announce his arrival. Horses were changed at the Saracen's Head, now with a much renovated façade; the figure of the White Hart stood not upon the roof as now, but on the ground to attract passing coachmen to its hostelry. Beaconsfield's thoroughfares were packed with inns. London End House, and the King's Head, which has the date 1741 on a rain-pipe, were formerly inns. There were many—the Prince of Wales, Elm Tree, Farrier's Arms, Plough and the Cross Keys—which are no more. In the 19th century it was because Disraeli travelled this way from Hughenden to visit Queen Victoria that he chose the name Beaconsfield on receiving a peerage.

Other travellers came through on foot. To those who were in need small sums were paid out quite regularly from the parish accounts. This was not entirely compassionate, for if a traveller died it was the liability of the parish to pay for his burial. So the sick might be given an offering to encourage them along to the next parish.

London End has carefully spaced limes dividing the busy road from a distinguished row of 17th and 18th century houses—Highway House, The Yews, The Old Post House, Malt House and Burke House (named after him; he lived at Gregories burnt down in 1813). At number one London End, a humble house of the 16th century overlooking the Market Place and now a shop, a series of remarkable wall paintings were discovered in 1966 and removed to the County Museum. On the walls of a first floor room were three figures: a young man wearing a soft "Rembrandt" hat, stockings tied at the knees and playing a lute; a man clad in a doublet and similar garb on his legs with a falcon on his wrist; and a less distinct figure of a woman in a long skirt holding a book or mirror. Mr. E. Clive Rouse suggests that they are the sophisticated work of an artist around 1600. The explanation for the presence of such ornate adornment in so modest a house is, as yet, unsolved. Anne Waller purchased the house in 1622–24 and it was retained in the family till 1811.

A row of venerable elms, a patch of green, the ornamental shrubs of Yew Tree Cottage, and roses at the foot of the permanently lit War Memorial make Windsor End the prettiest corner of the town. This was where the stocks used to be beside the village pond. Aylesbury End is also the Market Place; the centrally placed lock-up is now an Estate Office. Around the corner, in Wycombe End, I noticed, through the

39. *Windsor End, Beaconsfield*

modernised carriage-way of the George, a very old dovecote, and hidden away behind the Victorian church is one of the oldest buildings of Beaconsfield. Designed round three sides of a courtyard, black and white fronted with a generous use of timber, the Rectory House, built between 1500 and 1540, is considered to be an outstanding example of the architecture of its time. Lord Burnham, the journalistic pioneer of the 19th century virtually responsible for the raising of the *Daily Telegraph* to a leading position in Fleet Street, restored the building in 1901. It is now divided into three flats, and the lower rooms are used for parochial purposes.

A conspicuous stone obelisk on the tomb of Edmund Waller dominates the churchyard. Living at the time of Cromwell, to whom he was related, he was a poet with a ready wit whose changeable politics caused him to be severely judged by some. Born in 1606, he was the son of Robert Waller of Coleshill. In 1624, after his father's death, Edmund and his mother moved to Hall Barn Manor. He fell in love with Lady Dorothy, cousin to Sir Philip Sidney. It was a love not returned and to her he wrote the verse for which he is most remembered:

40. *Sir Edmund Waller, after J. Riley, c. 1685*

"Go lovely rose
Tell her, that wastes her time and me
That now she knows
When I resemble her to thee
How sweet and fair she seems to me."

He discredited himself with the Parliamentarians, and after the failure of "Waller's Plot" was banished to France. His poems, published in 1645 in his absence, influenced his return to favour. The diarist, John Evelyn, tells of meeting him in France in 1652 "as he had obtained leave of the Rebells (who had proscribed him) to returne". Appointed a Commissioner of Trade, Waller joined Milton, Dryden and Marvell in the small coterie of literati who received the patronage of Cromwell. Waller died in 1687 and the almost indecipherable lettering on his tomb suggest that he was considered to be the foremost poet of his age— "*inter poetas sui temporis facile princeps*".

In 1769, states an isolated remark in the *Victoria County History*, Beaconsfield was "only famous for being the residence of Waller". But in 1768, a far more influential figure had decided to make his home in Beaconsfield. Of Anglo-Irish extraction, Edmund Burke was said to be "tall, erect, well formed, but not robust in appearance, with a countenance of much sweetness, and in his youth was esteemed by some ladies

41. *Edmund Burke*

very handsome". One of the greatest political thinkers of the 18th century, he was a powerful man, renowned for his oratory, but less wise in the handling of his personal affairs. His purchase of Gregories for £22,000 left him in financial difficulties for the rest of his life. At his death in 1797 there was still a mortgage of £14,000.

Burke developed an affection for the town, liking to walk in the rural quiet of the woodland. His life ended in sadness, and after the death of his only son, Richard, from tuberculosis he wrote, "The storm has gone over me, and I lie like one of those oaks the late hurricane has scattered about me." He never recovered from the tragedy of losing Richard, whom others spoke of as vain and pompous, but whom he loved most dearly. By his own wish Burke was buried at Beaconsfield. In contrast to Waller, only a small brass plate in the church marks his burial place, and I moved a considerable number of hassocks before locating it, seventh row from the front, right-centre pews.

Another colourful figure joined the Beaconsfield scene at the beginning of the 20th century. G. K. Chesterton walked into the town one day with his wife and so delighted with it were they that they decided to leave London and make it their home. The year 1909 saw the arrival of Gilbert and Frances at a house called Overroads, where Gilbert lived until his death in 1936. Chesterton, poet, essayist, short-story writer and novelist, who always referred to himself as a "journalist", was quickly integrated into the Beaconsfield community. He took an immense delight in the people he met; barber, tailor, his doctor, Dr. Pocock, all became his friends. To Overroads came Eric Gill from nearby Piggotts, J. L. Garvin also living in Beaconsfield, Father O'Connor from Yorkshire, who was the inspiration of "Father Brown" the detective priest and other colleagues from Fleet Street.

The derivation of the name Beaconsfield remains open to question, and Chesterton was one of those who upheld the theory that it arose from the beech forests growing around it. To emphasise the point he often wrote "Beconsfield", as from the Anglo-Saxon "boc", or beech. More generally it is accepted as being an open space where warning beacons were lit.

From Beaconsfield a natural progression might be to Marlow, a town of undoubted beauty. "A bustling, lively little town" with "many quaint nooks and corners to be found in it" is how Jerome K. Jerome described it. But a book on Chiltern villages has not the scope to do justice to the attractions of the riverside towns, so instead we will move south-east to Burnham Beeches and Stoke Poges.

Covering a total of 600 acres, the Beeches were formerly owned by

Burnham Abbey. Founded as a House of Augustinian Canonesses by Richard of Cornwall, brother of Henry III, the original buildings still exist as an Anglican Convent. Prior to the Dissolution a loaf and a half bottle of beer was given each day to a poor person of Burnham "for the sake of the founder's soul". After becoming the property of Henry VIII, both Abbey and Beeches passed into the private ownership of the Wentworths, and in 1879 an area of the Beeches was bought by the Corporation of London.

The Beeches are traversed by avenues: several have been closed to motor traffic and even horses must maintain a seemly decorum and not gallop. Once the necessary notices and barriers of a mechanised age are passed it is possible to wander freely through one of the most remarkable collections of trees and shrubs in England. A lyrical, if unlikely, tale is told that at the end of each summer the nightingales flocked to Burnham from all over the country and united in a final concert before they flew south. More feasible is the suggestion that the area known as Egypt is so-named because it was much frequented by gypsies, or Egyptians, as they were once called.

The aged beeches, weird, uncanny, gnarled with great hollows and holes, have tortured branches emerging from gigantic trunks, some with a

42. *Burnham Beeches*

girth of over twenty feet. How old they are no one knows. Anyone may guess. They were already ancient when the poet Gray was staying with his uncle at Burnham Grove; his phrase "the most venerable beeches" having found its way into innumerable guide-books. The normal life of a beech is approximately 250 years, but these were pollarded again and again, probably for fuel, and the retarded, mis-shapen growth resulted. Disturb the layers of leaves about their roots, and a multitude of wood ants, attracted no doubt to the dying timbers, will appear.

These unique specimens of beech have a Mephistophelian look, but a single mature tree, and there are countless normal beech at Burnham, will reach a height of 60 to 100 feet. Each season finds the beech displaying a natural elegance. Late flowering, the massed beech have a purplish tinge, and as April turns to May, the new foliage upon the slender, lower branches is so delicately traced that it appears to be floating on air. Autumn brings radiance as the shades of the thick canopy of leaf range from brown to yellow, from orange to red.

Both Burnham and the nearby village of Stoke Poges have only just escaped the invasive growth of Slough. Every year thousands of visitors come to Stoke Poges from all over the world. Coaches spill out the latest

43. *The Five Bells, Burnham*

44. Churchyard, Stoke Poges

batch of sight-seers, with rapid steps they hurry through the lych-gate.
A guide with nimble tongue and lightning speed hustles them into the
church. Five minutes later, they crowd about Gray's tomb; cameras click,
a word from the guide, the coach re-fills and they are gone.

The attraction of Stoke Poges is certainly concentrated within the
churchyard. The popular view of the church seen through the lych-
gate has an undeniable charm. There are actually two gates, and the
long path emphasises how withdrawn is the church from the village. The
quiet of this corner of the Chilterns, where it is still possible to escape
"from the madding crowd's ignoble strife", is almost entirely due to its
being immortalised by Thomas Gray 200 years ago. Gray was born in
London in 1716, and was twenty-five when, following the death of his
father, a city scrivener, he and his mother moved to West End Cottage,
his uncle's home. Stoke Court now stands on the site of the cottage, the
"compact box of red brick with sash windows", where Gray lived during
his vacations from Cambridge. Most of the adult life of this reserved and
solitary man was devoted to the study of literature and the arts. He was
not ambitious, his own output was very small and few writers have gained
so great a fame by publishing so little. When offered the post of Poet
Laureate he refused it with some disdain. Beneath the dark yew, still

45. *Thomas Gray*

75

shading the porch of St. Giles, Gray is said to have composed the "*Elegy*". To remember that it took him four years to complete need not detract from the evocative picture of the poet in the shade of a very beautiful tree.

He did not marry, and our knowledge of his life contains only one vague indication of romance. Lady Chobham, wife of the Lord of the Manor, brought a young protégée, Henrietta Speed, to stay with her. A friendship sprang up between them and their young neighbour, and rumours of marriage were spread about. But the relationship between Gray and Henrietta, though genuine, remained platonic and later she married a diplomat, Joseph de Viry.

During his latter years, after his mother's death, he was reluctant to return to Stoke Poges and travelled widely throughout England. Ill-health overtook him, he had recurrent attacks of gout, and one day, after dining in Hall at Pembroke, he was taken ill and died when only fifty-five. An inconspicuous plaque attached to the church wall reads:

"In the same tomb upon which he has so feelingly recorded his grief at the loss of a beloved parent are deposited the remains of Thomas Gray.

The author of the 'Elegy written in a Country Churchyard'.   1771."

For twenty-eight years these brief words represented his only memorial. Not until 1799 was a decision taken to place a more imposing monument "amongst the scenes celebrated by that great lyric and elegiac poet". A colossal sarcophagus, designed by the architect Wyatt, was erected in the meadow known as Gray's Field. Maybe the shy poet who spoke of himself as "a shrimp of an author" would have turned his back upon the strange, tasteless monument, but at least it features a number of the immortal lines of his "Elegy":

> "Beneath those rugged elms, that yew-tree's shade,
> Where heaves the turf in many a mouldering heap,
> Each in his narrow cell for ever laid
> The rude forefathers of the hamlet sleep."

Separated from Stoke Poges by the green spaces of Stoke Common and Frame Wood is Fulmer. Traces of Roman occupation in the Chilterns occur mainly in the valleys below the escarpments; such a valley as the one through which the River Alderbourne flows on its way to join the Colne near Uxbridge. Here grew up the village of Fulmer. It is not a large village, and records indicate that it never was. The population in 1698, for instance was 84, and in 1969 about 700.

History records little about Fulmer before 1198, yet the discovery of ovens and a pottery kiln to the north-west have proved that settlers

46. Fulmer Village

were living there as early as the 2nd century. The presence of water is reflected in the name Fulmer, a variation of "Fowelmere", meaning "a bird-haunted mere", by which it was known in 1302. An area of marshy land, frequented by swans and moorhens, still exists on the north-western outskirts along Hay Lane towards Low Farm.

In mediaeval days the first church stood close to the mere. Not a salubrious position as the lord of the manor, Sir Marmaduke Dayrell, was to realise in 1610. This was the year when he had the good sense and the generosity to have it rebuilt on its present site where it shares the centre of the village with the Black Horse and the Village Hall of 1937. One bell, still rung as treble in a peal of six, and the solid main door are all that is known to have been transferred from the old to the new church.

When men were working on the new church (its red brick is a welcome variation from the local flint and stone) a temporary building was erected to accommodate them. It is believed that this may well have been the foundation of the 18th century Black Horse.

Sir Marmaduke, whose son, Sampson Dayrell, represented Wendover with John Hampden in 1626, died in 1631. There is no question of him being forgotten for an imposing monument, with effigies of Sir Marma-

77

duke and his wife, stands in the nave of his church. Lipscombe, in 1849, also noted his sword preserved in a chest beneath the belfry. This, and the pews "gorgeously lined with velvet", were lost during restoration work. The Dayrell Charity which included "4d. weekly and 4d. bread weekly to 6 poor people", and "12s. for gloves to the Dean of Windsor, the Junior Canon and the Rector of Fulmer" has been assimilated into the Fulmer United Charities. The Rector regrets the lapsing of the "more picturesque disbursements"!

On the wall of Webb's Cottage are the words "Kynd Kynn Knawne Keppe". On enquiring their meaning I was told it was the motto of the Kaye family who bought and rebuilt Fulmer Hall in 1820. Freely translated it is "Keep contact with your Kith and Kin".

The neighbouring Hedgerley, three miles north-west of Fulmer, is hidden in the folds of the lesser hills in as typical a "bottom" as can be found throughout the Chiltern range. Sloping to the road is a meadow where ponies graze, and a willow weeps over a pool. A garden rose is intertwined between the branches of an apple tree, and one mild October pale pink roses and bright red apples hung magically side by side. The church of St. Mark, just over 100 years old, sits upon the hillside over-looking the inn, the yellow washed walls of Dean Cottages, and the varying roof levels of Court Farm. Beyond is Church Wood, a bird reserve of the Royal Society for the Protection of Birds. Permission to visit is obtainable in the village. Although one of the smallest reserves, covering only 40 acres, the deciduous trees and dense undergrowth make it an excellent habitat for all woodland birds from warblers to woodcocks. A delightful field walk skirts the Reserve and crosses Bulstrode Park to the busy town of Gerrard's Cross.

From a few fragments of by-gone ages can be learnt a little of the people who made their way to, and lived in, Hedgerley. Excavations in 1935 discovered, as in Fulmer, two pottery kilns and ovens of the 2nd century. These first settlers made small bowls, dishes and jars; quite simple ones suitable for constant use, and mostly with a plain grey surface. An oven could fire 200 or 300 such small articles at a time. Within the confines of Bulstrode Park are traces of an Iron-age fort of 22 acres. And within the church is a brass of 1540 of Margaret Bulstrode, an ancestor of Bulstrode Whitelocke of Fawley, and her ten sons and three daughters. The brass is remarkable for being composed of several portions of other brasses, most probably stolen. On the reverse side is an inscription to Thomas Totington, an Abbot from as far away as Bury St. Edmunds in Suffolk. A framed remnant of tattered cloth hangs on the chancel wall. Devoid of embroidery, or rich embellishment, it is preserved with meticulous care as one of the historic treasures of Hedgerley. A story relates that King Charles II—though some attribute it to his father—visited Hedgerley and noting the poverty-stricken appearance of the bare altar, gave his cloak to be used as an altar-cloth. The one threadbare piece, proclaimed by experts to be of 17th century origin, is all that remains.

Lastly, not only is the date 1844 firmly inscribed on the outer wall of Church Cottage, but here too there is lettering—"Feed my lambs". However it is interpreted to-day, might this not have had a more immediate and urgent meaning in those days of famine, caused by the Corn Laws, known as the Hungry Forties?

CHAPTER V

Jordans to Ivinghoe

The Chilterns, once a deeply forested land mass cutting off London from the north-west, bred men who, encouraged by their relative isolation, were men of spirit who thought for themselves, and were not afraid to question authority. So when in the mid-14th century the Lollard doctrines of John Wycliffe were aired abroad it was characteristic that sympathisers were found in the area east of Oxford and towards London—Wycombe, Amersham, Chesham, Chalfont St. Giles. Wycliffe's preachers, barefoot and dressed in russet gowns, journeyed from town to town preaching in the churches, the street, or the market-place. Lollards believed in the direct relationship of an individual to God, attacked the Pope, the clergy and the worship of images. Convinced of the necessity for an English service in the churches Wycliffe completed, in 1380, the first English translation of the Bible but all through the 15th century any man or woman found with a copy was charged as a heretic.

Under a brutal statute of 1401 obstinate or lapsed heretics could be burnt at the stake, and when 20,000 Lollards marched to London, John Fynch of Missenden, Walter Yonge and John Hazelwode of Amersham were amongst the 39 who were martyred for their belief. Persecution was fierce and fear forced families to betray those they loved. A man who carried a faggot to a burning received 40 days of pardon. Punishments varied. Some did penance in the market-place, some were branded on the cheek with a hot iron and others wore a badge of green cloth as a sign of disgrace. At the burning of William Tylesworth of Amersham, his married daughter, Joan Clarke, was forced to start the fire.

The seeds of Protestantism were sown, and although Lollardism was officially suppressed, ordinary men and women throughout the villages of the Chilterns continued to meet in secret to study Wycliffe's Bible. When two centuries later George Fox and William Penn introduced the simplicity of Quaker beliefs they found hardly a village in the area which did not respond with its quota of enthusiastic supporters.

Jordans, four miles south of Amersham, is permanently associated with Penn, Isaac Penington and Thomas Ellwood. Isaac and Mary Penington were living at The Grange, Chalfont St. Peter (now a school) when the young Thomas Ellwood came on a visit, from Crowell in Oxfordshire, to find the whole family including his young playmate, Guli, had become Quakers. Within a year he too, against his father's wishes, had joined the new sect and adopted the Quakers' manner of addressing all men without any complimentary title, refusing to remove his hat, or bow his knee before any man. On the famous occasion when Penn kept his hat on in the presence of Charles II, the King removed his own as he explained it was the custom in that place for only one person at a time to remain covered.

Both Penington and Ellwood suffered periods of imprisonment and during one of Penington's enforced absences, in 1665, his wife, Mary, and her family were turned out of the Grange. With the help of Ellwood they found a new home at Bury Farm, Amersham. Ellwood and the lovely Guli were always friends and when in 1672 she married William Penn at King's Farm, Chorley Wood, it was "her true and trusted friend", Ellwood, who signed the certificate.

Wearing their own large-brimmed hats the first Quakers met in the Mayflower Barn at Jordans never knowing who might inform against them. In 1670 a meeting was disturbed with some violence by two informers. One was Ralph Lacy, a cow stealer, and the other a highwayman named Aris. Was it in spite of, or because of, their own lawless behaviour that they reported the Quakers to the Justice of the Peace, Sir Thomas Clayton of the Vache, Chalfont St. Giles?

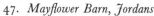
47. *Mayflower Barn, Jordans*

48. Jordans Meeting House

The following year William Russell, owner of Old Jordan's Farm, sold to Thomas Ellwood and others for £4 2s. 6d. a piece of land, Well Close Hedgerow, which is now the Jordan's burial ground. Later Russell's son sold a further four acres on which the Meeting House was erected in 1688 a year after James II granted his Declaration of Indulgence, which ended the persecution of Quakers.

Though not the earliest Meeting House in existence, the one at Hertford being a few years earlier, it is the most famous, and the most visited, especially by Americans. Secluded within a quiet valley, with white shutters framing the lattice windows, the plain brick house is fronted by a smooth lawn. In the grass are the simple headstones of William and Guli Penn, Penn's second wife Hannah and several of his children, Isaac and Mary Penington and Thomas and Mary Ellwood. Only the year of death is inscribed, the months being omitted due to the Friends' distaste for the pagan origin of their names.

. The meeting room is entered by way of the former kitchen, now a bookroom. Narrow wooden benches rest on a brick floor, and wooden panelling covers the lower half of the walls. Across the meadow is the Mayflower Barn. A cracked beam, the salt-impregnated timbers of its 90 ft. length, and the incomplete inscription "RHAR" form part of the evidence linking it with the ship in which the Pilgrim Fathers sailed from Harwich in 1620. In 1921 a single piece of the timber was removed and placed, as a token of friendship, on the Pacific Highway Association Peace Portal which marks the boundary between the U.S.A. and Canada.

Between 1798 and 1910 the Meeting House had not been used regularly, but from the beginning of the 20th century Friends began to settle in the neighbourhood. After considerable renovation Russell's farmhouse was converted to a hostel in 1912. A fire destroyed the old stabling and a long, timbered block of extra rooms has been recently completed. With the Barn and the house it forms three sides of a square to shelter and seclude the garden; a still quiet garden with mellow walls and steps, a sunken area with seats, a sundial, a minute pond and glimpses of wild cherry and spreading elm in the meadows beyond. A swallow flies into the Barn, and the doves, symbolic perhaps, decorative certainly, flutter over the historic roof.

Jordans village, designed by Fred Rowntree, took shape in 1919. Gabled red brick houses are set well back from the central green where silver birch and poplar grow. Beyond is the open space of Crutches Wood, given to the village in 1934 by Henry Cadbury and Baron Trent of Nottingham.

Twitchell's Lane moves north-east away from Jordans to meet the long road travelling down through Three Households (no longer just three) to return to the valley of the Misbourne and Chalfont St. Giles. Here trees fringe the near distance and a willow gives cover to the plump Muscovy ducks on the pond. The church, its grey tower seen above the roof tops, is reached under an archway and through an interesting swing gate operated by a rope and pulley. Old houses and new shops inter-mingle to face the green. Stacey's has a thriving vine. The name of the inn, Merlin's Cave, is said to have arisen from a cave in the meadow behind it. On the green is not only the appropriately eerie sign of the inn, but also the attractive innovation of a village sign designed by John Kendall to commemorate the Coronation of Elizabeth II. Sir Norman Birkett, High Court Judge and ardent conservationist, who lived at Challen's Green, spoke at its unveiling in 1953. The sign portrays St. Giles, patron saint of the Norman church, with his crozier and hind. Not a great deal is known about St. Giles for he lived a hermit-like existence in the forests of southern France before the 9th century. He owned a pet hind. One day it was hunted, but when the huntsman followed the arrow he had let loose he discovered it was Giles, who, in protecting his hind, had himself been wounded.

Chalfont, mentioned in Domesday as Celfunde, ceadeles funtan, a spring, was held at that time by Manno the Briton. Manno was an ancestor of the Wolvertons who held the manor until 1349. A second

49. *Milton's Cottage, Chalfont St. Giles*

manor originally belonged in 1166 to Warner de Vacca whose name is remembered in the Elizabethan manor house, The Vache. Here lived George Fleetwood, who in 1643 raised a troop of Dragoons to defend the Chilterns against the Royalists. He was one of the Parliamentarians who signed the death warrant of Charles I and was knighted by Cromwell in 1656. On the return of Charles II he was condemned to death. His life was spared, but The Vache was forfeited and eventually, in 1662, sold to Sir Thomas Clayton, the Justice of the Peace who acted harshly towards the Quakers. In the late 18th century Sir Hugh Palliser erected a monument in the grounds to his friend, Captain Cook.

Milton's Cottage, on the edge of the village, is the only one of the houses in which he lived still in existence. In July 1665, when London was beset by the Plague, Milton's young friend, Thomas Ellwood, who had read Latin to him in London, found him this "pretty Box" as a safe retreat. Ellwood's further words, though much quoted, are still worthy of repetition. It was he who said to Milton after his arrival at Chalfont: "Thou hast much here to say of Paradise Lost, but what hast thou to say of Paradise found?" Milton acknowledged his friend's thought later when he handed Ellwood a manuscript entitled "*Paradise Regained*". "This", he said, "is owing to you for you put it into my head by the question you put to me at Chalfont."

> "O what a multitude of thoughts at once
> Awakn'd in me swarm, while I consider
> What from within I feel myself, and hear
> What from without comes often to my ears,
> Ill sorting with my present state compar'd."

From February to October two rooms of the cottage are open every

84

50. *John Milton*

day except Tuesday; from November to January viewing is restricted to week-ends. Portraits, first editions and letters solely relating to the poet fill one room. He is to be seen as a boy of ten, and as a father with his daughters in a copy of Romney's famous portrait. A mixed and somewhat confused collection of items of local interest occupy the second room. Pillow lace, old maps of the county, cannon ball relics of the Civil War, a copy of Waller's poems and Ellwood's history of his own life all lie together in the little room. A rush-light holder recalls the economical and ingenious use of rushes in place of the more expensive candles. Rushes, gathered in the autumn, were prepared and dried, then soaked in scalding fat. Good specimens, just over two feet long, would burn for nearly an hour giving a good, clear light.

A pear tree spreads its branches over the outer wall, and bluebells, wallflowers and polyanthus flower in a garden, little changed, I felt, from when Milton sat there, a little lonely, perhaps, in his isolation from London. The cottage, only 60 or 70 years old when its one illustrious tenant rented it from David Fleetwood of the Vache, has since housed many occupants, including a tailor, wounded at Salamanca, who used to sit working at the long window overlooking the garden. In 1887 the Milton's Cottage Trust bought the cottage with Royal backing, Queen

Victoria making the first donation of £20.

Chalfont is linked with the fascinating and lovely old town of Amersham by a three mile stretch of the A 413. So nearly caught up in the development sweeping over the Home Counties, with a new town on the hill and a sausage factory at the London end, Old Amersham has still not lost the essential character of a mediaeval market town. It has had an eventful history. Domesday records it as Agmodesham, and under the provisions of a charter, granted to the town by King John in 1200, a market and fair was allowed to be held every September "for ever". The presence of dissenters was known from the 14th century onwards, and in 1521, after visiting Amersham, John Longland wrote of this "whole countryside where heresy had existed for generations in organised shape". His merciless inquisition resulted in 200 people being accused as heretics. As an example five men and one woman were burned on the crest of Amersham Hill, where the Martyrs' Memorial now stands.

A grammar school, founded by Dr. Robert Challoner, a rector of Amersham, was originally housed in the High Street. Dr. Challoner's School is now on the outskirts of the town, but the words "Grammar School 1624" may still be seen on an archway between shops near the Market Hall. A few years earlier, in 1602, a marriage was arranged between Joan Tothill, of Shardeloes, and Francis Drake of Esher, a

51. High Street, Amersham

86

member of the Inner Temple. Joan, a girl "of low well-compacted stature, and a lively browne complexion" married against her will and is said to have been beset by tempers. Believing herself to be damned she was constantly visited by divines to exorcise the evil spirits which she thought had overcome her. From this marriage of convenience is descended the long line of Drakes who virtually controlled Amersham up to the 20th century.

William, the elder son of Francis and Joan, was responsible for building the Almshouses in 1757; and dying, unmarried, in 1669 left bequests to his neighbour Waller, and Sir Ralph Verney of Claydon. The name of his brother, Francis Drake, occurs frequently in the Verney Memoirs, and it was his son, also William, who built the Market Hall in 1682.

The 17th and 18th century papers of Shardeloes, the home of the Drakes for three and a half centuries, have been admirably transcribed and annotated by Mr. M. G. Eland. Sir William Drake (1723–96), who undertook the rebuilding of the house, was one of the wealthiest commoners of his time, the father of four sons and four daughters. Eland makes the sad comment that he was also entirely devoid of humour. A dull man who, nevertheless, provided his descendants with a beautiful, lavishly decorated and comfortable home. He, when Shardeloes was completed, decided the air did not agree with him and retired to London!

From April 1758 until 1766 work was in progress on the renovation of Shardeloes. Stiff Leadbetter of Eton was the original architect, and its completion by young Robert Adam makes it his earliest work. Nearly a million bricks, 436,500 common stock and 430,000 large bricks for the outside fronts, were used; the white stucco was added later. The great hall is 30 foot square; towering trees form a backcloth to the long white façade and Corinthian columns of the porch. On the crest of a hill the house is magnificently situated. Groups of trees punctuate the turf reaching down to the lake. William Cobbett admired the parkland as he rode by in 1822: "Mr. Drake's is a very beautiful place and has a great deal of very fine timber on it." In the modern conversion of Shardeloes and the stable block into twenty flats and maisonettes the fireplaces and Adam decoration have been preserved.

At either end of the town, where the Misbourne puts in a brief appearance before vanishing under the road, is a Mill, one a private house, the other a restaurant. In the three quarter mile length between them are gathered the period houses and inns which overlook one of the finest mediaeval thoroughfares in England. Beginning from the London End on the corner of Gore Hill is Bury Farm where Mary Penington took refuge. On one of the first cottages in the Broadway is a faded notice, dated June 24, 1811, warning "beggars, ballad singers and other vagrants" against disturbing the peace. Across the road cottages of around 1700 have been metamorphosed into smart little shops. A fountain splashes into the waterlily pond of the Garden of Remembrance. Beyond the roses and the seats by the well-tended flower beds, the green hill curves up to the New Town.

At this point I have to say what a pity about the gasometer and pass on quickly to Sir William Drake's Market Hall. Patterned by the skilful use of Buckinghamshire purple brick it is a building of which any town would be proud. It displays the Drake Arms, and at one corner is a pump dated 1785; behind it is the old lock-up with a grille and a peep-hole. The bell in the charming wooden bell-turret is inscribed "C.H. made me 1682", which marks it as coming from the foundry of Christopher Hudson. There used to be a rope by one of the open arches with a notice saying: "In case of Fire the sum of one shilling will be paid to any person ringing this bell."

In the High Street dignified houses of the 17th and 18th centuries, opening on to the street, stretch out in an unbroken line. Many are topped by patterned and decorative early brick chimneys. Every now and then a high carriageway interrupts the continuity to offer an enticing

52. *Market Hall, Amersham*

glimpse of flowers and trees beyond. Amersham's trees are mostly behind the street. The ornamental cherry at the gate of Apsley House, and the pollarded limes guarding the almshouses are an exception. The six blue doors of the single-storied almshouses open on to a courtyard, and were intended "for the relief of six poor widows well reputed in this parish". In addition to their regular 6s. a week, they received a bonus of 9s. 4d. on the longest day, and 1s. 4d. on the shortest day, and a new gown every two years.

Of the numerous inns the black and white King's Head is the most picturesque, Cromwell is said to have dined at the Griffin, the Swan has 1671 on a chimney and the modern front of the Crown is deceptive for this 300 year old inn has suffered two disastrous fires. The magistrate's court used to be held in the bar, and a regular horse-bus journeyed between the Crown and the Old Bell in Holborn until 1890.

Facing the street, which because it curves round like a wheel to High Wycombe, is called Whielden Street, is the Tudor workhouse, one of Gilbert Scott's first commissions. It is now the Amersham Hospital. A sundial above a shop in the same street is said to be a copy of a very early dial of 1372, removed from the shop and now in Aylesbury Museum. Exploring Amersham will yield many further pleasures—the grey flint church, the yellow-washed Rectory looking down upon the town, and a scent factory in the premises of an old brewery. Last, but by no means least, there are the green paths running behind the town to some of the loveliest countryside the Chilterns have to offer.

As the name of Drake recurs throughout Amersham, so the very small and typically feudal village of Chenies and the Bedfords are inescapably linked. Despite its long association with the Russells it is to an earlier manorial lord that the village owes its name. Prior to the 13th century it was known as Isenhamstead, and from that time until the 16th century the Cheynes held the manor, and to Isenhamstead was added Cheyneys. Only as lately as the 19th century has the single Chenies been adopted. John Russell, the first Earl of Bedford, owned the village and surrounding lands from 1526, and it stayed in the possession of the Bedford family until 1954 when it was sold to raise money for death duties. Thus the Russells were the sole landlords for 400 years. It was Francis, the second Earl, whose inheritance of extensive lands in Cornwall, Devon and at Woburn in Bedfordshire, greatly increased the wealth of the family.

The Manor House is architecturally intriguing. Briefly, the west block, containing a tower, is probably 15th century, and the first Earl added the south wing about 1530. The extremely tall chimneys—there are seventeen on the south side alone—have varying ornamentation. Past

53. *Manor House, Chenies*

references to the house have called it Chenies Palace, and why not for both Henry VIII and Elizabeth I stayed here on more than one occasion. Henry's ghost is said to haunt the downstairs rooms where he slept on one of his visits when his leg was causing him discomfort.

Following the death of John Russell in 1555, a private chapel was added to the existing 15th century church. A glass screen divides the Bedford Chapel and its impressive array of monuments from the nave of St. Michael's. So at least we may look curiously through the glass and above the black and white marble floor see both ornate and beautiful memorials to the family who created Chenies.

Good agricultural land surrounds the village. "From Chenies, I passed much good pasture and corn ground", recorded Leland. The villagers who were dependent on the goodwill of the Manor were fortunate, when in the Victorian era of agricultural prosperity, the Bedfords rebuilt and improved the cottages of the estate. Proof of the Bedfords' generosity in the re-housing of their tenants lies in the comparatively large and well-designed cottages, all neatly arranged about the green. Each bears a date—1840's to 1850's mostly—and a conspicuous "B", and they all have an elegance rarely seen in small houses of that period. In 1846, Anna Maria, wife of the seventh Duke, built the school for the children of Chenies; church, school and cottages collected together under the aegis of the manor.

Old elms shade the roofed well, and carefully protected beech saplings have been planted amongst them. The bus shelter has a framed footpath map presented to the village in 1971 by Douglas Mackie, and at the residents' request, and by special concession, the telephone kiosk has been painted grey. This very special village is beautifully set in the wooded valley of the River Chess, and beyond Whitehill Cottage and the enormous Cedar of Lebanon at the gate of Chenies Place a by-road goes steeply down to the picturesque corner known as Chenies Bottom. The level of the Chess is high here and always seems about to spill over into the water meadows. There are cobblestones, cows, hens, doves, occasionally a donkey in the field, and a narrow lane climbing up between the hedgerows and on to Flaunden.

In the vicinity of the Chess Valley four sites, at Latimer, Sarratt, Chenies and Chorley Wood, have produced evidence of Roman Occupation. Mr. J. F. Head in *"Early Man in South Bucks"* suggests that there may even have been a local route of communication in the Roman era from the valley to St. Albans. Archaeological investigations between 1963 and 1970 have built up a detailed picture of a substantial Roman villa on the site of Dell Farm, Latimer. Among the discoveries were two roof tiles showing the footprints of a dog; he must have stepped on them accidentally before they were dry. Erected between A.D. 130 and 140 the villa had flint walls, and at first a single long corridor, or passage, with five or six rooms leading off. There was at least one small bathroom. Major re-building occurred sixty or seventy years later, and a comprehensive bath suite was added. The walls and ceilings were decorated in five colours; one room had a mosaic floor, and the courtyard was 200 ft. square. An outer wall surrounded it, and a roadway probably led out to the east. After being abandoned for a short while, it was re-occupied at the turn of the 4th century and more rooms were added to make fifteen or more. By the middle of the next century it was completely abandoned and there was no further building till modern times.

The outstanding feature of contemporary Latimer is Latimer House, now the National Defence College. The red brick mansion has looked down austerely over the valley for little more than 100 years, but before that there was "a fayer house" to which Charles I was brought as a prisoner. It so happened that his son was to seek refuge here as he made his escape to France.

Latimer has associations with Gilbert Scott. He was born in Gawcott, north of the Chilterns, and when in 1826 he was sent to study mathematics and architecture with his uncle, the vicar of Latimer, he found the district "hilly and delightful". In later years he remembered it as "a

54. *Latimer*

little paradise", and his feelings are shared by many who have an especial affection for the Chess Valley. After designing the Martyrs' Memorial at Oxford the industrious Scott quickly rose to fame and became the leading architect of the Victorian age. One of his numerous restoration commissions was the church at Latimer which he renovated in 1867.

Latimer's green, recently shorn of its elms which were victims of the 1971 epidemic of Dutch elm disease, is encircled by an intimate group of cottages. Bright gardens and white painted railings link them in pleasing harmony. Latimer has its village store and post office at April Cottage, but is that rarity, a village without an inn.

The population of Latimer in 1971 was only just under 100, as compared with the 21,000 of its near neighbour, the sizeable town of Chesham. Chesham's initial development was mainly due to the sawmills, and the boot and shoe trade. With its small pockets of industry, it does lack the charm of other Chiltern towns. Skottowe's Pond, with the view to the grey church framed by trees, glimpses of the Chess at Waterside and of the town's oldest cottages in Church Street are however rewarding.

Two interiors are of interest. In the reign of George I a painter decorated the walls of a small room in the George and Dragon in the High Street. Admittedly he was an artist of limited talent who painted for his own pleasure, and probably did not visualise his work coming under the scrutiny of experts 250 years later! He portrayed a primitive picture of a man with a long wig and a gold braided coat, and in his design of birds and flowers he included a fritillary, once not so rare as now.

A modern interior, designed to please and satisfy the public, is the Chesham library opened in 1972. It is spacious; its reference and student area is well stocked, well appointed and comfortable and it echoes the pattern of several of the recently built County libraries, as at Wendover and Great Missenden.

On the hill ridge radiating to the north-west of Chesham are a number of interesting hamlets. Hawridge and Cholesbury are twin villages which have shared a manorial history since 1704, and were united as one civil parish in 1934. Two small churches, one at each end of the parish, are both near the site of a pre-historic encampment. And over the centuries each village has expanded along the hill-top.

St. Mary's, Hawridge is hidden from the road and reached by the holly-edged driveway of Hawridge Court Farm; the camp-site is within the farmlands. A medley of houses and cottages keep to one side of the road as they string out along the ridge. The upland common of Hawridge merges into Cholesbury and only a boundary stone marks the division as a road branches off to the Hawridge-Cholesbury Mill. It first appeared as a smock-mill in 1863. When later its woodwork was thought to be

55. *Village Green, Latimer*

56. *Hawridge-Cholesbury Mill*

unsafe, it was re-built as a tower-mill. Since its role as a private house, it has red paint on its sails, and is very spruce and trim.

Gilbert Cannan, novelist and friend of Lytton Strachey and Dora Carrington, lived in the nearby Mill House during the 1914–18 war when it was a rendezvous for the literary Bloomsbury set.

The widening common attracts its own visitors, children, picnickers and cricketers. From the grounds of the church of St. Laurence a gate leads to a field bordering on the ramparts of the Iron-Age hill fort. About 10 foot high they are most clearly defined by a semi-circle of beech growing along the ditch below. Seven hearths were found in the central area. There is a belief that when the Saxons inhabited the 15 acre camp they baptised their converts in the nearby pond. It is to a Saxon, Ceolweald, that the village owes its name, Ceolweald's Burh, later Chelwoldesbye. A definitive account of the history of both villages is given by David and Joan Hay in *"Hill-top Villages of the Chilterns"*.

A mile to the north-west at the junction of the roads from Cholesbury, Tring and Wendover is one of the most attractive of all Chiltern churches. The low, white plastered walls of St. Leonards, quite dazzling through the trees, are a notable change from Chiltern flint and stone. There is a small bell-turret and above it a resplendent golden weather-cock. A recent innovation is the orange paint on the outer doors. Golden winged angels, bearing shields support the roof beams, and Humility, Truth and Courage are illustrated in the stained glass of the east window.

An absorbing history is attached to this unassuming house of worship. First records name a hermit, Leonard of Blakemore, who rented an acre of corn and an acre of grass for 7s. a year from the Manor of Aston Clinton. He is thought to have founded a cell, or small religious house. Whether he himself came from Missenden Abbey or from the old hospital of St. Leonards at Aylesbury is uncertain. The suggestion has been made that he founded the church. Joan and David Hay rather regretfully discard

94

this idea as in 1150, a few years before his arrival, the district already had a small population, large enough to have had some form of chapel. During Cromwell's regime the church fell into ruins and owes its restoration to the munificence of one of Queen Anne's Generals, Cornelius Wood. An unusual gathering occurred about 200 years later when nearly 300 gypsies, or "diddicoys" as they were often called in Buckinghamshire, came to this tiny church for the burial service of one of their tribe, Abigail Norris.

Five miles to the north of St. Leonards lies Ivinghoe, one of the northern bastions of the Buckinghamshire Chilterns. Sir Walter Scott gave the title "Ivanhoe" to his novel after remembering it incorrectly from the old rhyme:

> "Tring, Wing and Ivinghoe
> For striking of ye Prince a blow,
> Hampden of Hampden did forego
> And glad he could escape so."

What basis there is for the rhyme is doubtful for even if an ancestor of John Hampden did strike the Black Prince during some feat of chivalry, these three villages were never part of the Hampden estate. For whatever reason Ivinghoe is remembered its cruciform church of St. Mary, resembling a young cathedral, is unmistakable evidence of its former status.

57. *Thatch-Hook on Wall of Ivinghoe Church*

The fact that from the time of Edward the Confessor until 1551 it belonged to the Bishops of Winchester stresses its mediaeval significance. Geographically Ivinghoe's position, at the meeting of the Upper and Lower Icknield Ways, was such that many travellers seeking a route around the hills made their way through this agricultural town.

The importance of those days has vanished; contemporary activities take place in buildings built long ago for other purposes and a few of the earlier larger houses have disappeared altogether. A Youth Hostel is housed in "The Old Brewery", a splendid and dignified 18th century house. Next to it the Elizabethan Town Hall serves as a library. Firmly attached to the churchyard wall is a purposeful thatch-hook. Shaped like a giant crook, its wooden staff is bound in iron. In the event of fire, it was used to drag the thatch from a roof.

On entering the church the beauty of the interior is made doubly arresting by the light which flows uninterrupted through the clear glass. The nave wall bears circular traces of the Norman clerestory windows and there is wood carving of exceptional interest. Look from the roughly carved pew ends and the dark elaboration of the Jacobean pulpit to the splendour of the angels with outspread wings below the beams of the honey-coloured roof. On one of the pew ends is a mermaid combing her hair. She is probably not just due to the romantic thought of a mediaeval

58. *Ivinghoe Beacon*

59. *Pitstone Green Mill*

craftsman, but intended as a warning against the temptations of this life. Brass candle-holders swing out from the lectern, and on the pulpit an hour-glass is a reminder of the days when the length, if not the subject, of the Vicar's sermon was a regular topic of conversation during Sunday lunch. During the drastic Victorian restoration much else of antiquarian value was irretrievably lost.

Ivinghoe is resigned to the dwindling of its former importance and has settled back into a quiet, rural village renowned for the splendour of its church and the accessibility of its hills. A mile to the east is the impressive downland rise of the Ivinghoe Hills. Protected by the National Trust, they are ideal and much frequented terrain for ramblers, country lovers and model plane enthusiasts. The Beacon, a striking summit of 762 ft., is the "hoh", or spur, of "Ifa's people" from which the town acquired its name. From the summit there are panoramic views of the surrounding countryside stretching over Bedfordshire. You can see the striking Whipsnade Lion cut out of the Dunstable Downs, and look across the Aylesbury Vale to Oxfordshire. It can be very cold along the top, but it is surprising how rapidly shelter is gained by dropping just below the crest of the hills.

Just below the hills stands the Pitstone Green Mill, reputed to be the oldest post mill in England. In the early mediaeval post mills the entire building was set upon a tall oak post securely supported at the base, and enclosed by a round house, so that the whole superstructure, with its machinery, revolved to suit itself to the wind. The 17th century tower mills, as at Cholesbury, had a fixed main body of brick, or stone, and only the top cap swivelled round with the sails.

The first timbers of Pitstone Mill are dated 1627, and its working life was only ended by a storm in 1902. After that it was left to deteriorate, and not until 1963 did an awareness of its historic value evoke the raising of a public subscription towards its restoration. The work itself was undertaken by local volunteers, an example at present being followed by members of the Chiltern Society in the saving of the Lacey Green Mill.

Now in the custody of the National Trust, the Pitstone Mill is open on Sunday and Bank Holiday afternoons from May to the end of September. Sharing the skyline with the smoking chimneys of the Pitstone Cement Works the Mill remains in isolated dignity in the middle of a corn-field.

CHAPTER VI

Aldbury to Tring

The western arm of Hertfordshire, fitting into the Chiltern pattern like a jig-saw, contains the loveliest and most rural villages of the county. Aldbury, like Hambleden deep in the Buckinghamshire hills, and Checkendon beautified by the fine beechwoods of Oxfordshire, is a village which enjoys a special relationship with its immediate surrounding countryside. It is tucked closely into the foot of a steep chalk ridge from which spring the trees of Aldbury Common. To the west productive agricultural land sweeps away towards Tring.

For at least half the year the charm of the village is accentuated by its flowers, for although Town Farm and a number of the cottages open straight on to the road, not an inch of available earth is wasted. Roses ramble over weathered walls. A wistaria branches extravagantly across the front of the Greyhound. Wallflowers, japonica and aubretia bloom below the solid beams and lichened roofs of the 16th and 17th century cottages. An attempt was made to grow water-lilies on the pond, but I was told that "it wasn't used to them and they died", so the pond has been left to the martins and swallows which swoop across it in search of food.

The 300 year old timbered Manor House is close enough to be reflected in the water, and the well preserved stocks and whipping post stand on the nearby green. The ridicule of the stocks was once punishment for a multitude of sins. Some of which, such as playing games and travelling on Sundays, seem innocuous enough to-day. A common sight in every village for the 400 years between 1400 and 1800, they had fallen into disuse by the 1830's.

Facing the village centre is a curious little building in a cottage garden. It has a tall chimney and a small balcony housing an old well. Beyond is the grey tower of St. John the Baptist's where the repetition of family names in the three much commemorated great families of Verney, Whittingham and Duncombe is confusing. In brief, Pendley Manor, which lies west of Aldbury and is now a College of Adult Education, was the home of the Whittinghams in the 15th century. Sir Robert Whittingham, who died at the Battle of Tewkesbury in 1471, left an only daughter, Margaret. Margaret married John, a son of Sir Ralph Verney, Lord Mayor of London. The Pendley estates then passed into the hands of the Verneys of Claydon and it was Sir Edmund Verney who in 1575 constituted the Pendley Chapel in Aldbury Church for the express purpose of moving the family memorials to it from Ashridge.

Elsewhere in the church an unusually small brass depicts John Danvers, grandson of Sir Ralph Verney. A purse hanging from his belt suggests he was a merchant. Before the installation of the organ a pitch-pipe would have been used to lead the singing, and Aldbury's mahogany one is preserved in a glass case.

Aldbury was the home of Mrs. Humphry Ward. A novelist and one of the first women magistrates, she was the grand-daughter of Dr. Arnold of Rugby. She was born in Tasmania, came to England when only five and in 1872 married Thomas Humphry Ward who had bought the house called Stocks from Lord Grey of Fallodon. Very much a woman of her own time, her works, of highly emotional content, are little read to-

60. Manor House, Aldbury

day. In her novel *"Bessie Costrell"* the scene is set in Clinton Magna, otherwise Aldbury. A villager who as a girl worked for Mrs Ward, spoke of her as kind, gracious and charming to her work people.

Footpaths wander south over the fields to the Cow Roast at Wigginton; an inn whose name does not refer to some traditional barbecue but is said to be a corruption of Cow Rest, where drovers halted their cattle en route to the London cattle markets. Other paths wend their way up between the beeches to Aldbury Common. Actually there is a series of commons. Aldbury and Berkhamsted to the south, and to the north Pitstone from which an area of deciduous woodland, Sallow Copse, spreads towards Ivinghoe.

Much of the area, including the 3,127 acres of the Ashridge estate, is National Trust property, and the variation of common, park and woodland offer pleasant alternatives for leisure-time activities. It is, like West Wycombe and Burnham Beeches, a honeypot area, but that is only because those who visit it doubtless agree with the poet, John Skelton (1460–1529) who said, "a pleasanter place than Ashridge is, harde were to finde". Golfers and riders are well provided for, and walkers even more so. A multitude of footpaths criss-cross the whole district, golf course included. Some are signposted, some not. Horses may churn up patches of the bridleways, but at least they help to keep these shared tracks free of obstruction. Silver birches rise out of a bed of deep bracken; wild cherry yields a harvest of berries for the thrushes, and elder, Scots pine, yew, sweet chestnut, larch and many more, decorate the land. Here and there the beech again comes into its own.

61. *South View, Ashridge*

So cosmopolitan a collection of trees alone holds a delight, not only for the countless shades of green, yellow and red according to season, but also for the greater variety of wild life attracted to mixed woodland as compared with a pure beechwood. In places the thick undergrowth provides excellent cover for the smaller birds that choose low nesting sites—like the wren, and the visiting warblers, chiff-chaff and white-throat. Jackdaws send out their hoarse cries from the tree tops, turtle doves are heard, if not seen, and several species of tit fly rapidly through the branches. There is always the possibility that a deer will appear as if by magic, and vanish as suddenly into the shadows.

The story of Ashridge is peopled by a number of characters of varying degrees of fame. Its origins go back to 1283 when Edward, Earl of Cornwall, founded a house of Austin Canons. After being extended by the Black Prince in 1376 and undergoing the normal ups and downs of a monastic order, it reverted to the Crown at the Dissolution and became part of the estate of the Princess Elizabeth. Henry VIII's three children, Edward VI, Mary and Elizabeth, all lived here for a while. Elizabeth was at Ashridge, unwell and uncertain of her future, when Mary sent her Lords to bring her to Whitehall.

Early in the 17th century it became the home of the Bridgewaters, for one of whom Milton wrote the masque *Comus*, first performed at Ludlow Castle in 1634. The last Duke Bridgewater, and the most famous, was Francis Egerton. Born in 1736 he was a slight boy who developed so slowly that upon the death of his brothers there was a suggestion that he should be passed over in favour of a distant heir. Fortunately the idea was abandoned and at the age of twelve he inherited the title, and under the guidance of a perceptive tutor blossomed into an active man, owning and riding his own racehorses. After the breaking of his engagement with the widowed Duchess of Hamilton because of the scandalous behaviour of her sister, women were excluded from his house, even as

62. *Bridgewater Monument*

servants.

His conception of a canal scheme in the northern coalfields, and his meeting with James Brindley, whose practical ability made the plan possible, was the one far-sighted act of an otherwise eccentric man. Contrary to contemporary expectations the canals brought him a fortune, but he showed little interest in Ashridge until shortly before his death in 1803. He commissioned the architect Wyatt, but it was his heir, the seventh Earl, who saw the completion of the rebuilding. From the broad turf of the mile long Prince's Riding the monument to Bridgewater, a tall Doric column, is framed between the trees. I have not walked up the 172 steps to the top, but it may be done.

At the time of the Brownlows' inheritance of the property, water for Ashridge was obtained from a 13th century monastic well, 285 feet deep. Up to 1604 it had been operated by dogs, and afterwards by donkeys. Lord Brownlow remedied the somewhat inadequate situation by building in 1857, a waterworks for Little Gaddesden which also supplied Ashridge with main water. Beneficial as this was, it is said that in the 1920's the whole mansion had only two bathrooms.

The castellated walls, the turreted tower, the Gothic porch and the slim spire of the chapel are linked by the 1,000 foot frontage of Totternhoe stone. Architectural experts have frowned upon it, but it has a careless Gothic extravagance which is rather magnificent. Inside, the outstanding feature, apart from the chapel, is the great hall. Gazing down from niches beside the wide, stone staircase are nine statues—Edward, Earl of Cornwall and his parents, the Black Prince, Edward VI, St. Benedict, Bishop Canteloupe, Richard Watford (first Rector of Ashridge) and a monk.

Being now a College of Management, opportunities to view Ashridge are limited to the three Bank Holidays of Easter, Whitsun and August. Fortunately the gardens are more easily accessible, and may be seen during the summer months from April to August (afternoons only). Originally landscaped by Capability Brown, who always spoke of the "capabilities" of a site, they are reputed to be the most beautiful gardens in Hertfordshire. With the exception of the quiet seclusion of the old monks' garden, everything is on a grand scale. Avenues and groups of mature trees contribute to the lavish order of the design. The giant Wellingtonias are superb. Rhododendron time finds it ablaze with colour. Topiaried yew hedges, and the clipped cube-like box upon the terraces show a meticulous attention to detail. At all times the gardens are restful in their space, broad walks, smooth lawns and curving rose beds.

One of the interests of the nearby church of Little Gaddesden is the eye-catching array of monuments, accompanied by eulogistic epitaphs, to the Bridgewater family. The simplest and most apt is a line to the last Duke: "He drove his boats where farmers drove their ploughs."

The situation of St. Peter and St. Paul is attractively rural. Half a mile behind the road, it is surrounded by open meadowland. Inviting footpaths wander in all directions, to Badger Wood, to Ashridge and even to Whipsnade. The village is characterised by exceptionally broad green verges and well-established houses with mellow gardens. Behind the War Memorial and a wall of beautifully ornamented stonework is the mediaeval house still called "John of Gaddesdens". Pevsner suggests it is of 15th century origin and as John of Gaddesden was Physician to King Edward III in 1335 he cannot have lived in this particular house. The Manor House is Elizabethan. With mullioned windows and the entrance framed by an arch of yew it occupies the corner of the green. It was until her death, in 1971, the home of the musician, Dorothy Erhart. Pending a decision on its future, it is temporarily closed to the public.

Two miles as the crow, or any other bird flies, separate the two Gaddesdens. Great Gaddesden—it is a distinguishing rather than a definitive prefix—nestles at the foot of Piper's Hill. It is a village owing much to its hill-side position beside the River Gade, but little to its village plan. Haphazardly collected together are the very early church, the Cock and Bottle inn, and modern dwellings which seem to have been built without thought to the character of the existing earlier cottages. Wildfowl add life to the small mere, and I counted eighteen martins' nests below the eaves of the inn last summer. The Victorian letter-box, on a pillar half-way up the hill, is almost a museum piece having been placed there in 1861.

Long before the Normans laid the first foundations of the church 700 years ago, a Roman villa stood on the same site. At the back of the nave is a remnant of a stone pillar said to have come from the villa, and a few Roman bricks were incorporated into the present walls. There is also a heavy chest, hewn out of one solid piece of oak. The tiny slit in the top, which the Vicar believed was for Peter's Pence, suggests the chest is pre-Reformation work. The tax of a silver penny payable to the Pope was, of course, abolished in the reign of Henry VIII. An epitaph to Thomas Halsey who built Gaddesden Place, tells us that "owing to the instability of human felicity he was only able to inhabit his new house for fourteen years".

A modern story is attached to the organ. In 1971, when badly in need of repair, it had been put to rights by the gift of parishioners. All was well, and the music of the church was as it should be—for one Sunday only! Then came torrential rain, and, as the water came through, the discovery that lead had been stolen from the roof. The newly repaired organ was newly damaged. Dismayed, but with good will, the small congregation encouraged various endeavours, including sponsored walks and a sponsored skip, which helped to raise the sum once again required.

Also on the outskirts of the village are Gaddesden Row and Waterend. At Gaddesden Row a handsome array of flints, tools and weapons used by our Stone Age ancestors was discovered. At Waterend the river widens, and is crossed by a shapely bridge. Enhanced by trees and a scattering of brick and timber cottages Waterend is acknowledged as a minor beauty spot.

Three miles south-west of Great Gaddesden is Berkhamsted; the town to which, whatever way we had conducted this tour of the Chilterns, we would have come eventually, as the Normans did after crossing the Thames at Wallingford. At Berkhamsted, the Saxons, under Edgar Atheling, at last submitted to the powerful Norman armies of William, who promised to be "a kind lord to them".

William gave the manor to his half-brother, Robert, and a castle was established on the northern slopes of the Bulbourne Valley. Until the end of Henry VII's reign Berkhamsted Castle was the home of royalty, lords and archbishops. Edward III's son, the Black Prince, brought his wife, Joan of Kent, to Berkhamsted. Legend has it that the Order of the Garter was created after the beautiful Joan, formerly Countess of Salisbury, had dropped her garter at a ball in Calais.

The 14th century found Geoffrey Chaucer as Clerk of Works under Richard II, though probably not as a resident. But after the death of Cicely, Duchess of York, in 1495, the Castle was abandoned and over the

63. *Waterend*

years was allowed to fall into ruins. At the beginning of the 19th century the main gateway and part of the southern defences still existed, but were demolished to accommodate the railway in 1837. It is only since 1930 that the Castle site (now open daily) has been under the care and attention of the Ministry of Works and Public Buildings.

All that is left of a once formidable fortress are isolated fragments of flint walling with ragged edges. Beech tower above the moat, primroses and daffodils flower on the high ramparts, and wooden steps climb the steep side of Shell Keep. The outer courtyard, 450 ft. long and 300 ft. wide, is a smooth green lawn, and at one end of this historic site is a pretty gabled house where the keeper lives.

Beorghamstede, once a homestead on a hill, is now a considerable town with a population of over 15,000. Berkhamsted has undergone the usual variations in spelling, and even now the comparatively recent omission of an "a" from the previous Berkhamstead is not always observed. If you do not wish to be identified as a stranger, refrain from stressing the middle syllable as locally it is always Berk'amsted.

Canal, railway and High Street run parallel with each other through the valley. Raven's Lane and Gravel Path are worth finding as they lead to the canal and the peace of the tow-path. Plain little streets now, but both of ancient origin. Raven's Lane was named after the family of John Raven, a servant of the Black Prince, and it was by way of Gravel

64. Canal at Berkhamsted

65. *Berkhamsted School*

Path that gravel from the Common used to be transported.

Perpetual traffic blurs the impression of the long High Street. A picturesque corner remains where, side by side, we meet the quiet of the noble church of St. Peter, with the timbered Court House behind it, and the youthful exuberance of the boys of Berkhamsted School. The 400 year old school was founded in 1541 by John Incent, Dean of St. Paul's, and the church is especially remembered for its association with the poet, William Cowper. He is portrayed in the east window, at his writing desk and accompanied by his tame hares which, owing to the building of a new sanctuary, are partially obscured.

Cowper's connections with Berkhamsted cannot be fairly separated from the story of his life, so touchingly revealed in his own poetry and letters. In 1728 the Rev. John Cowper, rector of Berkhamsted, married Anne Dunne, a descendant of Dr. Dunne, the poet. Three years later, on November 15th, their son William was born, and Berkhamsted, little more than a large village, was where he spent the only six completely happy years of his life. The "Pastoral House" was just a typical, prosperous and comfortable 18th century household, yet a home Cowper never forgot. Seeing little of his father, he spent much time with his mother who protected and reassured him. When she died, the six year old boy, lost and sorrowing, was boarded out at a school in Markyate on the Hertfordshire/Bedfordshire border. He suffered two years of utter misery before being taken away. Later as a pupil at Westminster, where one of his favourite friends was Sir William Russell of Chequers, he was happy and enjoyed the return to Berkhamsted where he walked happily through the lanes and commons with his father. In 1756 he left the Hertfordshire village for good, but the memory of the rural landscape remained with him always:

> "For I have loved the rural walk through lanes
> Of grassy swarth, close-cropped by nibbling sheep."

A period in London studying law caused such a depth of depression that he attempted suicide and was confined for a while in Dr. Cotton's Home for Madmen at St. Albans. It was after his recovery that he met and formed a lasting association with Mary Unwin. Mary, eight years older than he, cared for "Mr. Cowper", as she continued to call him, with unwavering good sense and a growing fondness, at Olney and then at Weston Underwood. He did suggest marriage, but an attack of insanity supervened and the subject was never mentioned again.

Surprisingly, it was only just prior to his fiftieth birthday that Cowper really began his serious career as a poet. In naming one of its roads Gilpin's Ride, Berkhamsted has kept green Cowper's association with the town. Not one of his poems is more diverting than the story of John

66. *William Cowper*

WILLIAM COWPER.
1731 — 1800.

Gilpin, "that citizen of credit and renown" who took a ride to Edmonton and was carried on to Ware. Cowper was fifty-eight when quite unexpectedly a cousin sent him a portrait of his mother, and the memory of his Berkhamsted home was revived. He remembered the "Pastoral House" and how the gardener, Robin, took him to school each day "wrapt in scarlet mantle warm, and velvet capt". But Cowper had no liking for travel. He never re-visited the place of his birth, and died in 1800 at the age of seventy-one. From a man who sought sanctuary rather than experience came the poetry, inspired by the country and the homely details of every day life, which has become part of our literary heritage.

"God made the country, and man made the town.
What wonder then that health and virtue, gifts
That can alone make sweet the bitter draught
That life holds out to all, should most abound
And least be threaten'd in the fields and groves?"

Berkhamsted has been the home of a number of celebrities in differing walks of life including the historian G. M. Trevelyan and the author W. W. Jacobs. Graham Greene was a pupil at Berkhamsted School. William Cooper, a veterinary surgeon who came to the town in the mid-19th century established a chemical works which now has world-wide connections.

In an age when protests on problems of environment are the order of the day two earlier instances in Berkhamsted are worthy of re-telling. The King's Arms, the town's largest inn (the Swan dating from 1607 is the oldest) has, during its 200 years existence, been the centre of many local events. Meetings of the Turnpike Trust and Petty Sessions were held here, and it housed the Post Office during the 18th century. One of its most uproarious gatherings was in 1833 when the local inhabitants protested strongly, but in vain, against the coming of the railway.

The second incident was both successful and of much longer duration. Lord Brownlow, on inheriting the Ashridge estate in 1866, made the mistaken decision of enclosing one third of Berkhamsted Common by erecting a heavy iron fence around it. Such an act brought inevitable consequences. Mr. Augustus Smith, owner of a nearby estate, in association with Lord Eversley, Chairman of the Commons Preservation Society took immediate and drastic action. Within the short space of a fortnight they organised a party of 100 men, equipped with stout tools, who travelled just after midnight from Euston by special train to Tring. The well-ordered expedition marched the three miles to Berkhamsted, and by dawn the same day every railing was laid upon the ground.

Litigation resulted and lingered on for four years, but at last judgment was given wholly in favour of Mr. Augustus Smith and enclosure of the common was forbidden.

Tring, five miles north-west of Berkhamsted, lies on the path of Akeman Street (A 41), the Roman road from St. Albans which hastens on through Aylesbury to Cirencester and the West. Known as Treung in the days of King Alfred, it has a Norman church with carved faces below the battlements and a 15th century stair turret. Edward II granted market rights to the town and a further charter in the reign of Charles II prescribed that straw plait be sold in the mornings, and corn in the afternoons. The 17th century inns, the Robin Hood and the Bell, and the even earlier Rose and Crown, recall the coaching era. During the 19th century silk mills provided a thriving industry, giving employment to men, women and children. By 1900 trade was not flourishing. Silk throwing was more or less finished, and local straw plaiting had also become a craft of the past.

That to-day Tring has become a mecca for naturalists is not immediately evident from the confinement of its narrow streets. Set on the edge of the 300 acres of Tring Park is The Mansion, where it could be said it all began. Built in the reign of Charles II, for Henry Guy, The Mansion was owned at one time by Sir William Gore, first Director of the Bank of England. The year 1872, when the Rothschilds bought The Mansion, was a memorable date in the history of the town, for from then, until the selling up of their estate in 1938, the Rothschilds were renowned for their generosity to Tring. The pleasant row of timbered houses in Park Street was built for workers on their estate.

An avenue of sweet-scented limes approaches The Mansion and the parkland rises up to Park Wood. The Hertfordshire County Council has bought up a large area of the woodland for preservation, and paths wind their way between the magnificent chestnut, oak and beech. There is an obelisk in the wood which bears no inscription, and is known locally as Nell Gwyn's Monument. The legend that she once stayed in The Mansion, and so might have walked this way, seems to have little to substantiate it. But, of course, she did, for a time, live not so very far away in the lodge of Salisbury Hall near Tittenhanger.

Lionel Walter, the second Baron Rothschild, not only began a natural history collection of insects in a small cottage on the estate, but also introduced a few exotic creatures including cassowaries, kangaroos and zebras into Tring Park. With the exception of the edible dormouse, introduced to the Park in 1912, and now breeding locally, these are there no more. Unfortunately this species is regarded by naturalists as a menace to the survival of the British dormouse because they are bigger and compete with it for food.

From this initial interest grew the Zoological Museum which he bequeathed to the British Museum of Natural History. Noted for its unrivalled collection of mammals, birds and reptiles of the world the friendly little museum in Park Street is open every afternoon, including Sundays. A vast modern extension for research has just been completed at the back of the original museum, and will rank as one of the principal ornithological centres of the world. Towards the end of June the profuse white blossoms of four North American calalpa trees beautify the entrance to the museum. Their pale, succulent-looking leaves dislike intense cold, and at the first frost of winter there is a spectacular fall, and the tree is bare, practically over-night.

Tring's attraction for naturalists does not end with Tring Park and the Museum. In addition there are the lake-like expanses of the Tring and Wilstone reservoirs. Constructed as reserves for the Grand Union Canal, they have some natural banks much frequented by both professional and amateur bird-watchers. One of the Nature Trails, which are an increasing and popular feature of the countryside, may be followed at Tring. This one is a mile in length and guides are available on the Reserve at week-ends. Originally aimed at children and young students, Nature Trails have quickly found a wider range of enthusiasts.

Standing on the bank by the Wilstone Reservoir, and I must admit somewhat frozen, for reservoirs are invariably cold, I was fortunate enough to see a pair of great-crested grebes performing their elaborate courtship ceremony. A ceremony which has intrigued the most experienced ornithologists. The two birds went through a ritual of crossing bills and "kissing", raising themselves up in the water in a kind of "penguin dance". As a token of his courtship the male bird brought a straggling piece of weed to his mate as an offering.

We cannot leave Tring without mention of William Cobbett. The dinner given for him in 1829 at the Rose and Crown inn is part of the town's history. So impressed was Cobbett by the "entertaining and hospitable company" that he addressed them for an hour and a half. "Everything", he said, "at this very pretty town pleased me exceedingly."

OXFORDSHIRE

CHAPTER VII

Chinnor to Stonor

The south-eastern tip of Oxfordshire which comprises the Oxfordshire Chilterns is stamped with a distinct personality of its own. In the west, especially around Ipsden, the fields are larger, sweeping down from the horizon to the edges of the road. Hamlets and villages appear at random, and by the Thames the villages have blossomed into affluent towns like Henley and Goring.

The area resounds with evocative names—Rotherfield, Maidensgrove, Russell's Water, Nettlebed and Bix. There is Checkendon, composed and very much alive amidst pure beechwoods as fine as anywhere in the Chilterns; Swyncombe with an early Norman church, remote and still beside the meadows; Bix and its Nature Reserve, and little Stoke Row guarding its unique *pièce de résistance*, The Maharajah's Well.

Even the signposts are different. The bold green and white signs which both Buckinghamshire and Hertfordshire use to indicate the direction of their footpaths have vanished. Their place upon the landscape has been taken by oak posts with black lettering. Solemn little posts which merge into the background. The Chilterns as a whole have 1,500 miles of footpath, made up of 3,304 paths. That they are recognised as the best maintained footpaths in the whole country is mainly due to the tireless efforts of the Chiltern Society since its foundation in 1965.

From the Thames at Goring Gap the hills rise to travel northward and follow the high western ridge through to Bledlow on the Buckinghamshire border. Just short of the county boundary, and tucked into the foothills below the chalk quarries are the villages of Chinnor and Crowell.

An ample supply of water from several springs encouraged settlers in Chinnor as early as the 4th century B.C. By Domesday the manor was held by Lewin, an English royal servant, and in 1279 there were about 70 tenants of the manor. Its position on the Lower Icknield Way made it very vulnerable during the Civil War, and troops sacked and burnt the village in 1643. A second disaster occurred in 1685 when a fire swept through the thatched dwellings. The churchwardens in that year gave money to 108 people who had suffered losses. In the 17th century evidence of the way crops flourished in the fertile soil is provided by the fact that the rector kept six tithe barns for the storing of wheat, barley, beans, peas, oats and hay. Amongst the carters, husbandmen, carpenters, tallow-chandlers, publicans, and graziers, we find in Chinnor, at the end of the 18th century, a gingerbread maker. He must have been both a good cook and a good teacher, for his son left Chinnor to make and sell his gingerbread in London.

Gradually the facts reveal the evolving pattern of Chinnor's development from a small agricultural village. By 1851, the number of men employed on the land was 141, and already 101 were employed in "trade". This included the Buckinghamshire craft of chair-turning. So the village grew and industry developed rapidly. By 1951 Chinnor, which had 862 inhabitants in 1801, had almost doubled its population.

In the High Street a few mellow houses, the heart of the original village, remain. Chinnor, seemingly enveloped by the industrial aura of its cement works, is still met by open country on all sides. Beyond the neat churchyard, Chinnor Hill, clothed by trees, breaks the south-eastern sky.

67. *Chinnor Church, John Hotham*

No peering into the gloom, or furtive searching under lengths of carpet is necessary to see Chinnor's picture gallery of brasses in St. Andrews. In 1935 the thirteen brasses, for which the church is famed, were removed from their original positions on the floor and set into the north and south walls of the chancel. An outstanding figure in this striking array is John Hotham, a Provost of Queen's College, Oxford. The engraving of 1361 shows him stern-faced, hands clasped and dressed in his outdoor cloak.

Detailed descriptions of all the brasses and the sixteen very large pictures of the saints by Sir James Thornhill, sergeant-painter to George III, are thoughtfully provided for visitors.

Chinnor's near neighbour, Crowell, has always been, and still is, a very small village. Its total acreage of 996 acres has not changed since Anglo-Saxon days. Watered by a little stream called the Pleck it had only 40 dwellings in 1851, many of which were destroyed by fire in 1859.

The Catherine Wheel, an hospitable little inn which re-appeared quickly after the fire, and the Norman church, stand back to back. A farm, a few cottages, the 16th century Ellwood House, and that is Crowell, the birthplace of Thomas Ellwood. He gave rather an exaggerated view of his native village when he referred to it as "a little country town".

The Ellwoods of Crowell were conservative and highly respected gentlefolk. Thomas, born in 1639, was their youngest son. Sometime before his second birthday, at the advent of Civil War, the family moved to London as a place of greater safety. Only when peace returned did the Ellwoods return to their native Crowell. Thomas, like Hampden, attended the Grammar School at Thame, but his father found it necessary for Thomas' education to be curtailed in order that his elder brother might finish his studies at Oxford. The brother died, whilst still a young man, leaving Thomas as the sole heir.

68. *The Catherine Wheel, Crowell*

After his father's death and following one of several periods of imprisonment for his Quaker beliefs, Ellwood had to sell the Crowell House. He spent the rest of his life, first with the Peningtons and after his marriage to Mary Ellis, at Hunger (now Ongar) Hill. Ellwood's place in history has been secured by his association with the great. He regarded Milton as "his master", Waller as "his courteous friend", and the Peningtons almost as his own family.

A later occupant of Ellwood House was Dr. Richard Fellows, Professor of Physic at Oxford. Handmade bottles, for which he was famed, were discovered in the garden.

Leaving Crowell to its memories the road (B 4009) continues. On the southern horizon the Stokenchurch Radio Tower rockets up from the miles of beechwood like a giant totem pole. Skirting Crowell and Aston Hills we come first to Aston Rowant and then to Shirburn.

Once Aston Rowant was a very large parish indeed, as until 1895 it included Stokenchurch and covered an area of 6 miles or so. Gaining its name from the Rohants, the manorial lords, it grew up beside the Holbrook. Until the 18th century the main route to London, the *Via Regis*, passed Warren Farm which was then the Drum and Plough inn. The re-direction to the west, said to be "more commodious to the public", took place in 1824.

The railway came, and before it closed in 1957 Aston Rowant Station was featured in two films of the 1950's, "*My Brother Jonathan*", and "*The Captive Heart*".

To-day prosperity emanates from the very old and the very new alike. There is Aston Park Stud, Plowden Park, new and expensive, and in the Manor House grounds there are nursery gardens. I found the broad green knee deep in buttercups and cow's parsley. Modern development has radiated from the green, whereas the original village was mostly confined to Church Lane. There it is that we find thatch, dormered windows, flint, and weathered walls. Everywhere there are pretty gardens and trees—chestnut, copper beech, cypress, lime. It is a pretty village, and a quiet one.

Light fills the early mediaeval church of St. Peter and St. Paul. A 13th century stone staircase, once the way to the rood loft, leads from the nave; the Purbeck stone font is of the same period. There is bright mediaeval glass, including an angel playing a harp. A wall memorial to Lady Cicill Hobbee (died 1618) delights with its gay reds and blues. The upraised face of Lady Cicill has doll-like rosy cheeks.

Aston Rowant's churchwardens' accounts include, as other parishes do, regular payments for pests—polecats, sparrows, hedgehogs and, less often, stoats. Such outgoings are interspersed by personal items affecting the welfare of the villagers. A handful of individual entries for the years 1731–2 include:

"Gave to a great belly'd woman"		I	O
To ringers on Gunpowder Treason		2	6
Paid for the King's Coat of Arms	3	7	6
For Withs, Ledgers and Sprays		I	6
Half a thousand nails		2	IO
Spent at Tetsworth going to a whory daughter		I	O

Shirburn has a moated castle and a 600 year old church, a 200 acre park, beechwoods, and a hill rising to 835 feet. From this village came men who gained a place in English history. Shirburn Castle, which dates from 1377, was the home of the Puritan family of Chamberlain between the 15th and 17th centuries. In 1716 it was sold to the Earl of Macclesfield who altered it considerably, and there have been Parkers at the Castle ever since.

The Earl's father, Lord Chancellor Macclesfield, an eloquent speaker, was known as Silver-tongued Parker. Because George I was unable to speak English, it was Parker who delivered the King's speeches for him. But his position as a favoured minister was not to last. He was found guilty of profiteering in the sale of high offices. Public disgrace and a period in the Tower followed the exposure of his corruptive practices. His career was at an end. He died in 1732 and was buried at Shirburn.

His son was highly regarded throughout Europe as a distinguished astronomer. An observatory was built at Shirburn and the Earl trained John Bartlett, a shepherd, and Thomas Phelps, a village stable lad, as his assistants in the science of astronomy. Phelps, obviously a well-chosen pupil, was one of the first men to discover the Great Comet of 1743.

The Earl, then President of the Royal Society, was instrumental in the

69. *Aston Rowant, Nature Reserve*

framing of Lord Chesterfield's 1752 Bill which introduced the New Style Calendar. The loss of eleven days caused much consternation throughout the land. But in the same year Macclesfield held a feast for 300 freeholders of Watlington and was consequently referred to as "the darling of all Oxfordshire". To the Castle he brought a valuable library including early English books, and letters of Sir Isaac Newton.

A great attraction to passing motorists is a small nursery stall on the corner of the quiet cul-de-sac leading to the Castle. Castle and church practically adjoin, but the church, for all its sylvan setting, has a worn and weary look and our view of the Castle is restricted to a gateway and rather dull chimneys.

From the steep heights of Shirburn Hill, the highest point of the Oxfordshire Chilterns, the views are panoramic. Footpaths lead up from the village, and at a wide gap in the hedgerow we can look down across the Icknield Way to the Oxfordshire Plains. On this ridge is the Aston Rowant National Nature Reserve, a protected area of 250 acres, including parts of Beacon Hill and Bald Hill. Picnic areas, nature trails and the wide views attract a steady flow of visitors. Whitebeam and juniper grow on the scrub, and the chalk is famed for its orchids.

Returning to the road (B 4009) we will move on by way of Watlington and down Firebrass Hill to arrive at Ewelme. To convey a lightning sketch of the village of Ewelme, Leland's mid-16th century description can scarcely be faulted: "Ewelm, an uplandish village—tooke name of a great poole afore the maner place and elmes growing about it.----The praty (a favourite word of Leland's) hospital of poor men is hard joined to the west end of Ewelm Paroche Church. In the middle of the area of the hospital is a very fair well".

The village is set like a rare, untarnished jewel of mediaeval heritage in the folds of the hills. It is a village full of green corners; grassy banks, patches of cow's parsley, apple trees, lilac, willow; even the village industry is green—the cultivation of watercress. Cottages are set here and there facing this way and that. Rows of elms still enclose the meadows; but being, though well-loved, a treacherous tree, the churchyard line was felled in 1947 for reasons of safety. Since the 17th century Ewelme has been noted for its watercress beds which stretch out from King's Pool and through the centre of the village for about a quarter of a mile.

Many names in Ewelme are self-explanatory. There is Rabbits' Hill, Beggarbush Hill and Cow Common, Chaucer's Court and King's Pool. The Pool, which is fed by seven springs, owes its prefix to a Lady-in-Waiting who was rash enough to push Henry VIII into it. The Shepherd's Hut does not allow us to forget that, although since the beginning of the

19th century pigs and cattle have become more profitable, the Chilterns once rivalled the Cotswolds in the rearing of sheep.

Tiles have replaced the thatch of the Duchess of Suffolk's almshouses. The almsmen no longer wear cloaks with a red cross, and in the thirteen, now beautifully modernised, houses of the Cloister, they each have two rooms and the care, should they need it, of a resident nurse. Almshouses and school share the same foundation date, 1437, which gives the school its status as the oldest church school in England. Lessons continue in the original building erected for the village children to be taught "freely without exaccion of any schole hire", but since the Education Act of 1944 it is a State Aided School. The headmaster still uses the old Grammar Master's room above the porch, and classrooms have been provided by the construction of a floor dividing what was once a simple, very lofty hall.

Occupying the highest position of the village, the Church of St. Mary has escaped the damage of war and "restoration". Its exclusion from the wanton destruction of the troops of the Civil War was due to the prompt action of Colonel Francis Martyn, an inhabitant of Ewelme. He was a Parliamentary officer, and on the arrival of the Roundhead soldiers issued an order that the key of the church should be withheld. His command was obeyed, and the superb work of the 15th century craftsmen was left unscathed.

70. *School at Ewelme*

The most notable feature of this exceptionally fine church is the elaborate alabaster tomb of Alice Chaucer, Duchess of Suffolk, who until her death in 1475 was one of the most influential women of her time. To Ewelme she gave church, almshouses and school. She is represented in life, in the habit of a nun and wearing on her left arm the Garter which she had been granted the honour of wearing in 1432. At the base of the tomb is a shrouded figure representing the Duchess in death. On the roof of this final compartment are two frescoes. Having undergone various contortions I gave up the attempt, but understand that by lying flat on the floor and aided by a favourable gleam of sunlight, it is possible to see them.

Alice, daughter of Thomas Chaucer, Governor of Wallingford Castle and a Royal Chief Butler, was the grand-daughter of Geoffrey Chaucer, the poet. Already a widow at twenty-four, she married William de la Pole, Earl of Suffolk. The Earl died a violent death at sea when their son, John was only seven. John married Elizabeth Plantagenet, and was held in high esteem by Richard III, but it is with the name Chaucer that they, and Ewelme, are for ever associated.

Also in St. Mary's is a sad, brief epitaph to Lord Andover's only son, John, written by Edmund Waller. Remembering the small boy's anxiety to reach manhood Waller said:

> "'Tis no wonder Death our hopes beguiled,
> He's seldom old that will not be a child."

In 1927 Ewelme became the last resting place of the novelist and humourist, Jerome K. Jerome, author of the inimitable "Three Men in a Boat".

East of Ewelme, beyond Cow Common, is Swyncombe, reached by one of the tortuous lanes wandering through this part of Oxfordshire as if more suited to a farm cart than a car. Swyncombe has no real village. The school and tidy houses by an open, natural green constitute the hamlet of Cookley Green in the parish of Swyncombe. It is a place of great antiquity. The name, which has undergone innumerable alterations—Suincumbe, Swycom, Soncomb, Swimcomb—relates to the valley where wild boar were hunted.

From 1086 to 1410 Swyncombe belonged to the Abbey of Bec in Normandy. The monks came across the channel and built the small stronghold, dedicated to St. Botolph, as a witness to their Christian belief. Throwing sunlit reflections on to the formidably thick, bare walls are windows of heraldic glass illustrating the manorial history from the days of the monks till 1732.

A single bell hangs under a gable on the wall, like a school bell, and inside the church we have the rare opportunity of seeing a bell of the 14th century at close quarters. The slightly damaged "Jesus" bell is in honourable retirement on a window sill. The words *"Hujus campane Ihesus est nomen speciale"* are worn with age, but the lettering is a work of art.

Swyncombe House, with its tall Tudor chimneys, and St. Botolphs keep close company in considerable seclusion behind a screen of elms and yew. Snowdrops and aconites create patches of white and gold in the solitary graveyard, and pigs move ponderously in the adjacent fields. This lonely corner of Swyncombe, unaffected by nearly 800 years of war and peace, wears the dignity of age and strength.

Russell's Water lies a mile east of Swyncombe. The water, that is the pool, borders the road, and the old kiln house of the Russell's brick-works has been converted into an attractive private house. Looking much modernised too is the ancient Beehive Inn tucked away some 50 yards off the road.

Another attractive inn, made gay with hanging baskets, is the Five Horseshoes. We pass it on the way to Maidensgrove Common, so it seems to be in Pishill, but just to add to our confusion it is, in fact, in the parish of Swyncombe. The high, breezy common is a popular place.

71. Swyncombe Church and Bell

Suddenly, after the shaded lanes and thickly canopied beechwoods, there seems to be a bonus of sky! Children come, adults too, with kites, model planes, anything that flies; cars come laden with picnics, chairs, tables and the paraphernalia of an alfresco meal. An interesting survey in 1972 disclosed that the majority of picnickers move no more than seven yards from their cars. But from Maidensgrove, as from everywhere else in the Chilterns, there are footpaths leading in all directions. A pleasant walk of less than a mile follows a well-defined track travelling down from the common to enter the Warburg Nature Reserve.

Scattered to the south of the common are several 18th century dormer-windowed cottages and the earlier Maiden's Grove Farm. Short lanes go hither and thither, ending at a farm or a cottage. The road continues, cutting through the woodland and down between the meadows to Stonor.

Stonor, sheltered by the stony, wooded slopes of a steep escarpment, is another in this series of Chiltern hamlets. Farmland patterns the valley slopes to the south. To the north are the "fayre woods" and hills of Stonor Park. Six miles from Henley, it was, until 1896, known as Stonor with Assendon. It is the 300 year old Upper Assendon Farm, facing an innocuous modern development, which bounds the southern extremity of the village. Grouped about the Stonor Arms are the older cottages. Stonor's almshouses were damaged by a German bomb which fell here in 1941.

The village does not extend very far, and it is only 300 yards north of the inn that we meet the gates of Stonor Park. There is no mistaking the inclination of the obvious footpath for it has been trodden out to give unrivalled views of the house, the grand sweep of beech on the horizon and the well-spaced parkland trees. The mellow brick house is withdrawn; its generous proportions being skilfully moulded into a fold of the hillside. Both house and chapel have origins going back to around 1280 when Sir Richard Stonor made it his home after his marriage to Margaret Harnhull. Enlargements and restorations have taken place over the centuries, and the interior of the flint-faced chapel was restored during 1959–60. Both John Piper and Osbert Lancaster advised on the re-decoration, and infinite care was taken to reproduce the 18th century colours as closely as possible.

It was in 1834 that Thomas Stonor became Lord Camoys, and it is still the Camoys' family home. Catholic priests are known to have found a hiding-place within these walls in mediaeval days. One of them, Edward Campion, used a secret printing-press to launch counter-attacks on the Protestant reformers. An act which led to his eventual death by execution.

I have never been this way without spotting at least one or two of the many fallow deer for which the Park is famed. They are a wild herd, varying considerably in size and colour. Some look almost black, whilst others range from brown to pale cream. The fur darkens in winter, at which time, as in the breeding season, they move in mixed herds. At other times of the year the bucks and does segregate themselves into separate parties. Silently, they merge into the thickets. If startled, they leap rapidly over the grass; and there are few more graceful sights than a party of deer bounding through the park in search of fresh cover.

CHAPTER VIII

Henley to Goring

The remaining area of the Oxfordshire Chilterns lies south-west of the A 423, bounded roughly by the triangle formed by Henley, Nettlebed and Goring. Having one of the most beautiful stretches of the Thames as its southern boundary, and being avoided by the major roads, it is singularly remote. Leafy lanes cut through the beechwoods. Heaths and commons are sprinkled with hawthorn and the gold of gorse and buttercups. Springtime, and the bowing branches of the cherry display their snowy blossoms. Just occasionally the arable land, specially around Ipsden, has expanded into larger fields sweeping up the foothills. Only a solitary field maple, or a hawthorn, marks the line of a vanished hedgerow.

On the Thames, Henley flourishes, gay and bright by its own beautiful and eventful reach of the river; a town to which superlatives are justifiably applied. Each year since 1839 Henley has been the scene of the world's most famous regatta. Spanning this fashionable stretch of the Thames are the low, graceful curves of Henley's bridge, built in 1786 to replace the earlier one swept away by the flood waters of 1774. On the keystone of the bridge is the mask of Isis, carved by Anne Damer and possibly modelled on her friend, Miss Freeman of Fawley Court. While Isis looks upstream, it is Tamesis who gazes downstream.

Boats await the leisure time of their owners; in Henley the place to be is on a boat. Alternatively, an excellent viewpoint from which to admire the whole river scene is the group of seats alongside the Angel Inn.

So on, too quickly perhaps, but as we are here more concerned with the hills than the river, we leave the town. From the Old White Horse the road, which owes its conception to Gainsborough's brother, Humphrey, rises towards Bix in one superbly landscaped Fair Mile. An addition of the 1930's is the neatly named inn, The Fox at Bix, a much frequented stop for users of the Henley to Wallingford road (A 423). Nearby the village post office looks too small and retiring for its position on a busy highway. It is because of the highway that Bix is a disconnected little place. Situated south of the road is the Manor Farm; a timbered house, with barns made beautiful by the patterning of herring-bone brick. Only a few yards from the rush of the traffic, the farm wears the dignity of time and careful preservation. To the north a single-track road leads to the village school, now a private house, the comparatively recent church, a small development of houses and a broad open field. On the far side of the field relics of Roman habitation were discovered.

Bix—its odd name is derived from the Old English, bynce (box wood)— has had, since 1967, an area of 247 acres in the dry valley of Bix Bottom preserved as the Warburg Nature Reserve. Owned by the Berkshire, Buckinghamshire and Oxfordshire Naturalists' Trust (B.B.O.N.T.) it was named after the Oxford botanist, Dr. E. F. Warburg, and is especially noted for its rich collection of chalk-loving flowers. Founded in 1959 the B.B.O.N.T. has been very active, and by 1972 had control of no less than thirty-seven reserves in its endeavour to conserve and preserve the flora and fauna of the three counties. These include areas of the Chilterns at Dancers End, near Tring, Chinnor Hill, Hodgemoor Wood at Chalfont St. Giles, Park Wood, Bradenham and Braziers End, near Cholesbury. Not all of them are open to the public.

Having left the Fox at Bix the A 423 cuts through the forest of beech

72. Henley Bridge

73. *Brick Kiln at Nettlebed*

which is Nettlebed Wood. Not forgetting the cool shade of its green canopy, nor its autumnal warmth, this particular avenue is at its most impressive in April, just before the fresh leaf is seen. Then, as the budding branches merge above the road, Nettlebed is approached through a haze of purple.

Situated 700 feet up on a spur of the hills, Nettlebed, at the junction of the roads from Henley (A 423) and Reading (A 4009), is a village with a brick kiln and a narrow and unremarkable main street. Scenically its reputation rests on its immediate environment; the woods of the Nettlebed estate, Windmill Hill (the mill was burnt down in 1912), and the open fields sloping down from the church to Howberry Wood Farm and an easily recognised line of Grim's Dyke.

Brick-making has been a feature of Nettlebed for many centuries. The antiquarian, Dr. Plot, remarked in 1677:

> "About Nettlebed they make a sort of brick so very strong that whereas at most other places they are unloaded by hand, I have seen these shot out of carts after the manner of stones to mend the roads, and yet none of them broken."

Stones, or flints, for mending the highways used to be gathered by the women from the fields after the harvest, and then put into piles by the roadside for the repair work for which, by law, the men of each village were responsible.

A further impression of Nettlebed just over a hundred years later is also worth recalling. To this hill-top village travelled Karl Phillipp Moritz, the German professor who made a tour of southern England on foot, carrying a copy of Milton in his pocket. Walkers, such as Moritz, were regarded with suspicion. Those who did not arrive by coach, or on horseback, must be vagrants, evaders of the law, or beggars. Several inns turned him away, but the proprietor of an inn at Nettlebed, no doubt a perceptive man, provided him with a room without hesitation. So welcoming was his reception that Moritz stayed on in this friendly village for several days.

South of Nettlebed are the Rotherfields. To introduce them it is as well to explain the derivation of their names. Rotherfield, which is rarely used locally, is merely open land where cattle, "Hryther", graze. Leland making his meticulous notes said of the one village: "It is of moste men called Rotherfield Gray by cause that one of the Gray of Ruthyne came to be the owner." Similarly, Rotherfield Peppard was once owned by a French family called Pipart.

Greys village consists of The Maltser's Arms, a small church the Normans built, fine elms and chestnuts and a handful of houses grouped about a bend in the road. Displayed in the famous Knollys Chapel is a comparatively recent discovery—a set of scales and titheweights. Made by Swithin of London they are the oldest surviving set in the country. In the Chapel lie the effigies of Sir Francis Knollys and his wife, who was the niece of Anne Boleyn. Kneeling on top of the canopy are the figures of their son, the Earl of Banbury, and his wife. At the foot are two rows of serious-faced sons and daughters. The lavish golds and reds present a reminder of the colourful Elizabethan age. Anyone so inclined might well pass an hour or so working out the relationships on the collection of memorials within the Chapel! It must be enough here to say that Sir Francis, who died in 1596, was a good friend and courtier to Elizabeth I, who called him "an honest man". Less likeable a personality it seems was his son, the Earl of Banbury, on whom it is believed Shakespeare based the character of Malvolio.

For the four centuries following the Conquest, Greys Court was the domain of the de Greys. Only after the presumed death of Francis, great grandson of the 5th Baron, following the Battle of Bosworth, did the family line come to an end. So alongside the castellated dwelling grew up the home that was to belong to the Knollys for the next four centuries. During the reign of James I, Greys Court was connected with an event

74. Grey's Court

considered at the time to be one of the most sensational on record.

Frances Howard, sister-in-law to William Knollys, was both beautiful and unscrupulous. She was a frequent visitor to the Knollys' home. Having obtained a divorce from the Earl of Essex, she found her proposed marriage to Robert Carr opposed by his friend and adviser, Sir Thomas Overbury, the poet. Overbury was thought to have knowledge which would ruin Carr, and by employing devious means Frances managed to have Overbury consigned to the Tower. Whilst held there as a prisoner, Overbury died. Shortly afterwards Frances and Carr, now Earl of Somerset, were married. Two years later the Somersets were accused of Overbury's murder by poison. She confessed to having been instrumental in the mixing of poison into Overbury's food. Despite her husband's protestations of innocence, they were both convicted. Having been detained in the Tower, they were pardoned, but sent into confinement at Greys Court.

Only as recently as 1969 have the historic house, the picturesque ruins, and the 280 acres of gardens and grounds been donated to the National Trust by the present owner, Sir Felix Brunner. From April to September inclusive, the grounds are open to the public every afternoon except Sunday. Parts of the house, where Sir Felix and his wife still reside, may be viewed on Monday, Wednesday and Friday afternoons only.

There is a touch of pageantry about the scene as the elegant grey house gazes directly over the sloping lawn to the Tower and Courtyard wall— all that remains of the mediaeval home of the Greys. Only white flowers and shrubs grow in the Tower garden; fragile blossoms against enduring walls.

The house is set in undulating ground, giving delightful pastoral views. But it is within the gardens that there are some very individual trees. Japanese Cherries flourish by the Tithe Barn. A rare weeping ash and the generous splendour of a tulip tree are to be found by the Dower House, and the larch to the north-west of the house is believed to be one of the oldest in England. Its aged branches touch the ground.

On a wall beside the house stand four small cherubic figures. Each wears a helmet, set at a rakish angle and carries a weapon in play rather than earnest. Inside the house there is delicate 18th century plaster work on ceilings and walls. Far more utilitarian is the earlier kitchen with its hefty beams and sturdy oak staircase. Possibly it may have survived from the Greys' original home.

Although the hills are lower here, there is a fresh and breezy air about the two miles of tree-lined road which leads to Peppard. On the way are a pair of attractive hamlets. Greys Green is a gathering of pretty houses about an extensive green. On the far side is a forge, and the house nearby used to be the village post office. Once they both faced the school. But that too has moved away, and Cherry Tree Cottage stands in its place. Alongside, well back behind their carefully tended gardens, is an attractive row of pensioners' houses. No shop, no school: but there is still, so a pensioner told me, cricket on the green.

Half a mile away at Shepherd's Green I found the post office. Here the green is tucked away from the road and it is only past the plain, square inn, called The Green Tree, that we come upon a scene of picture-postcard prettiness. Roses creep towards the thatch; clematis winds over white walls and there are long views to tree-tops beyond. Two paths have been cut across the green where modest field flowers grow. There is sorrel and sturdy plantain, pink clover, yellow cat's ear and the tiny hop trefoil.

The Oxfordshire Chilterns are bounteously supplied with greens, but at Peppard we find a Common. Roads have split it up here and there, but from certain angles there appears to be no break in the broad, unmown turf dotted with buttercups and white hawthorn. It is countrified, satisfying, and, at week-ends, popular.

A "No through road" notice heralds, as so often, a quiet destination

75. *Stained Glass at Peppard*

129

where tall limes scent the lane and a field path continues on. The church, for all its Norman origin, has a perky appearance as, topped by a bell-cote, it is framed by trees. Modern stained glass in the west window depicts, rather dramatically, a ship in full sail. Subtly blended shades of brown, cream and palest yellow upon the pulpit, altar and reredos look, from a distance, as if painted. They are, in fact, inlaid olive wood dyed to produce the required shades. Madonna lilies and passion flowers adorn the pulpit, and the reredos is a copy of da Vinci's *Last Supper*. It is all the expert and delicately fashioned work of Mirabelle Grey, sister of Charlotte Knollys and wife of Major Grey, cousin to Earl Grey of Fallodon. When she died in 1922, at the age of 79, the whole village grieved, for she was much loved.

All situated within a few miles of each other, these villages are connected by long, winding lanes, the loveliness of which it is difficult to convey. They tunnel below the deep shade of the beech, for the beechwoods seem never-ending. A raised bank may reveal the trees' shallow roots, showing clearly how difficult it is for other growth to compete with both their canopy of leaves above, and radiating growth below. Holly is its most common companion, but in May, bluebells, so much more graceful growing than picked, create a carpet of blue. There are hedgerows with

76. *Maharajah's Well, Stoke Row*

stitchwort, the ubiquitous cow's parsley, red campion, and occasionally chicory of a blue even brighter than the bluebells.

These lanes, and Joanna Cannan in her book on Oxfordshire goes so far as to call them "diabolical", can be disconcerting. The villages, civilised as they are, are still astonishingly difficult to find. But that is part of their attraction for they encourage the feeling of being in the depths of the country.

So it is by various meanderings and a wrong turning or two, that we arrive at the comparatively straight Stoke Row, a straggling little place on the way to Checkendon.

Stoke Row is distinguished by the most unusual of village sights, The Maharajah's Well. Now gated off as an item of historical interest, it was, when presented to the people of Stoke Row in 1864, a purely utilitarian gift. The water supply of the village, in common with other upland villages such as Stokenchurch, Peppard and Turville Heath, was very uncertain. Around the middle of the 19th century Edward Anderdon Reade, one of the Reades of Ipsden House, having undertaken an engineering project for the Maharajah of Benares, happened to tell him of the problem of this English village. His story prompted the Maharajah to give the well as a token of friendship to Reade, and as a mark of his own understanding of the hazards of water shortage.

Whoever wrote the epitaph on Edward Reade's headstone in Ipsden church had a sense of humour for the single line reads:

"Be not weary in well doing."

The 350 foot well is a delightful oriental creation. The yews flanking the path appear to be approaching a small temple, for the well is surrounded by a little decorated tower, and a cherry orchard completes the background.

No one who has visited Checkendon just over a mile south-west of Stoke Row, could deny that it has an atmosphere of secluded charm.

Secluded is not necessarily synonymous with sleepy, and Checkendon is obviously a lively and a growing community. With great pride one of the older inhabitants said to me, "We are very proud of our village, come back and see it in the spring." The cherry blossom which beautifies Checkendon then is reflected throughout this corner of the Chilterns.

Closely gathered together are church, Checkendon Court set amidst formal gardens, and the humbler timbered cottages. I questioned the eye-catching irregularity of one of them. "Built crooked," said my friendly informant, "about 300 years ago." And 300 years is nothing in a village as old as Checkendon. The year 1972 is the 750th anniversary of the first record of a rector at the church of St. Peter and St. Paul.

However, according to conjecture, partially supported by fact, it was not the first church to be erected in the village. Some time after A.D. 634 St. Birinus, who had converted the Saxon King to Christianity, established a little church at Berins Hill, about one and a half miles away. Birinus had a neighbour, Caecca, and it does seem possible that he too was won over to the new belief, for there is evidence of a wattle and daub church in Checkendon about that time. Indeed the village may have Caecca to thank for its name. Another, and more poetic theory is that it was once Cecaden, a hidden vale.

The majestic Norman arches and the overall plan of Checkendon church bear a distinct resemblance to that of Swyncombe. In all probability the monks from Bec in Normandy, having completed Swyncombe, also built this second church just five miles away. Mediaeval murals surround the altar. There are early brasses, and a wall tablet remembers Admiral Manley, one of the first Englishmen to sail round the world with Cook. Fitting harmoniously alongside these relics of the past is a striking contemporary window, the work of Laurence Whistler. The design is cut into clear glass by Whistler's own technique of diamond point engraving and shaded sand blasting. Between the figures of *Probitas* and *Virtus* are a wheatsheaf and a chalice; here and there a star shines. The simplicity of the window is extraordinarily effective, but, if not viewed from a favourable angle, it is possible to miss it altogether.

No one in the neighbourhood would have missed Checkendon's contribution to the history of bell-ringing made on February 28th 1970. On that day a new peal, "Checkendon Surprise Major", was rung. The exact time taken to ring the 5,056 changes was 2 hours and 47 minutes.

A further three miles of lane brings us to Ipsden. Quite a spectacular three miles as the woods give way to open country and far-reaching views over Wallingford and the rest of Oxfordshire. There is a noticeable expansion of the fields. The questionable uprooting of hedges, which was never very prevalent in the Chilterns, seems to have come to a halt. Fortunately the majority remain intact for a hedgerow may be as much part of our ancient heritage as the stone or brick of an historic monument. It is not as simple to date as a building, but there is an old rule-of-thumb method by which it is said the approximate age of a hedge may be calculated. Select a 30 yard length of a chosen hedgerow and count the varying species of shrubs in it. The number found will equal the hedge's age in centuries. For instance if hawthorn, elder, crab-apple, cherry and whitebeam intermingle in a chosen length the hedge may be about 500 years old—a hedge of Tudor origin.

Ipsden continues the association with St. Birinus, for it was once

Biseden, the hill of Bishop Birinus. It is an indeterminate village. A single shop accompanies a few, as yet, unseasoned bungalows. The 800 year old church stands alone with a formidable array of yew dividing it from the wide, open fields.

Ipsden House was the home of the Reades. The writer Charles Reade, who died in 1884, is best remembered for his historical novel, "*The Cloister and the Hearth*". His comment on his Ipsden home was hardly complimentary, for he said it was probably "the coldest house in Europe". But that was about 100 years ago. His "*Hill Stoke*" in "*The Woman-Hater*" is undoubtedly Stoke Row, which he remembered more happily as being a village of 1,000 cherry trees.

Where the hill slopes away from the house to a meeting of minor by-ways is a gnarled and hollow pollarded elm. Though looking ready to rival the beeches of Burnham it is probably much younger, for elms rarely live over 500 years. It shades a timbered granary supported by twelve staddle stones. The grain, and it could hold enough for twenty horses, was thus protected from rats.

Across the road is the remarkable barn of Ipsden Farm. The farmer claims that, at 365 feet, it is the longest barn in England. An occasional brick bears initials and a date. The earliest I saw was "T.R.1766"; and other dates, 1770, 1806, 1811 are clearly cut on inner beams. The later dates may well refer to repair work, and there are literally thousands of beams supporting the whole structure. Up-to-date harvesting machinery is now housed between these venerable timbers; tractors in the stables, a combine harvester and vast corn silos in the barn. The massive double doors, painted red, are high enough for a loaded cart to enter, but the double doors are not so essential in these days of mechanisation. When the grain was threshed by hand with flails the through draft blew out the chaff and dust. I watched the house martins collecting scraps of mud from the yard and flying straight through the wide gap to build their nests on the ledges of the timbers.

To the west of Ipsden the Icknield Way travels directly to Goring and the Thames. Goring is a typical, if smaller, edition of several pleasant Thames-side towns. It is cheerful and bright. Creeper festoons the Miller of Mansfield as it curves into the narrow High Street. But the heart of the town is the river, and the usual activity surrounds the lock; gates move slowly, water fast, boats await their turn. Invariably there are spectators.

The Icknield Way has made its way here to cross the Thames to Streatley and Berkshire. Upstream the river flows to Oxford. Downstream to London. To the north-east are the Chiltern Hills through which we have come. Hills and valleys where the best of the gentle English countryside is still to be found. Where ancient villages, very much alive, vie with each other in the charm of their enduring appeal. To these villages, although written in another connection, William Cowper's words might be fittingly applied:

"Scenes must be beautiful, which, daily view'd,
Please daily, and whose novelty survives
Long knowledge, and the scrutiny of years.
Praise justly due to those that I describe."

Bibliography

BECKINSALE, R. P. *Companion into Berkshire.* Spurbooks, 1972.

FRASER, MAXWELL. *Companion into Buckinghamshire.* Spurbooks, 1972.

ELAND, G. *Shardeloes Papers of the 17th and 18th Centuries.* Oxford University Press, 1947.

HAY, DAVID and JOAN. *Hilltop Villages of the Chilterns.* Phillimore and Co., 1971.

HEAD, J. F. *Early Man in South Bucks.* Bristol, 1955.

JENKINS, J. G. *Chequers.* Pergamon, 1967.

JOHNSON, W. BRANCH. *Hertfordshire.* Batsford, 1970.

KEMP, BETTY. *Sir Francis Dashwood.* Macmillan, 1967.

LELAND. *Itinerary.* Centaur Press, 1964 ed.

LIPSCOMBE, G. *The History and Antiquities of the County of Buckinghamshire.* 1847.

MARTIN, F. *The Thames Valley.* Spurbooks, 1972.

MARTIN, G. *Chiltern Churches.* Spurbooks, 1972.

PEVSNER, NIKOLAUS. *Buildings of England—Buckinghamshire and Hertfordshire.* Penguin, 1960.

Records of Bucks. Bucks. Archaeological Society.

Victoria County History of Buckinghamshire, Hertfordshire, Oxfordshire. Oxford University Press, 1902–64.

WARD, MAISIE. *Gilbert Keith Chesterton.* Sheed and Ward, 1944.

Index

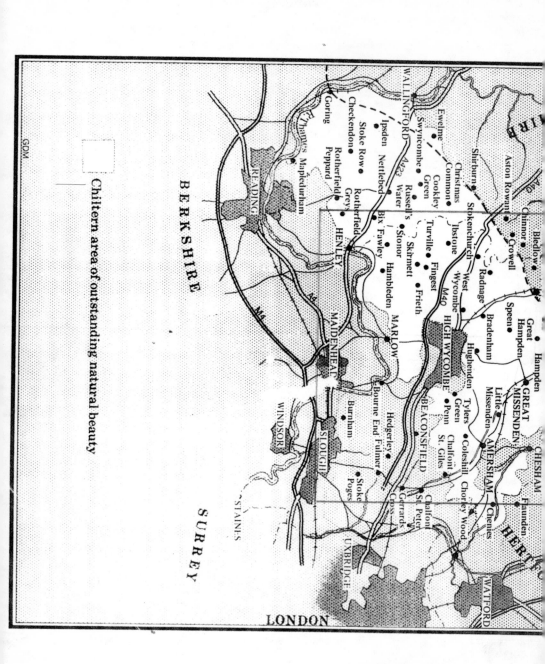

Chiltern area of outstanding natural beauty

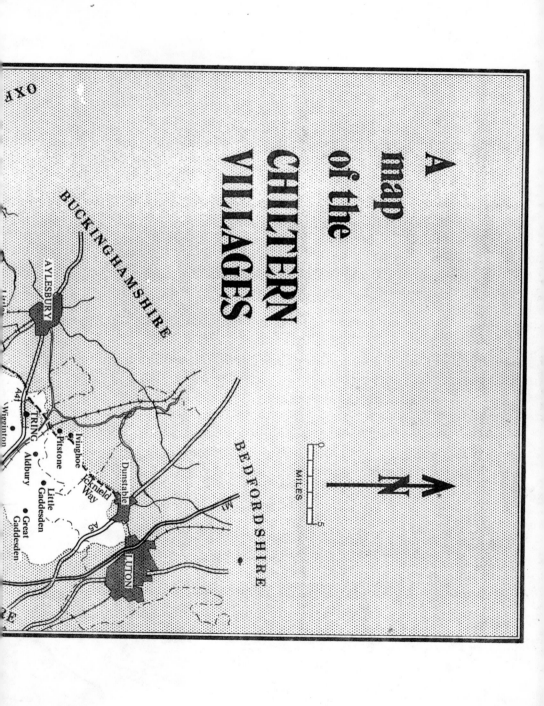

A
map
of the
CHILTERN
VILLAGES

N

MILES

OXON

BUCKINGHAMSHIRE

AYLESBURY

A41

Wigginton

TRING

Pitstone

Ivinghoe

Little
Gaddesden

Aldbury

Great
Gaddesden

Icknield
Way

Dunstable

A5

LUTON

BEDFORDSHIRE